OFF TO FIGHT
Young Heroes of History

by
Alan N. Kay

WHITE MANE KIDS
SHIPPENSBURG, PENNSYLVANIA

This White Mane Books publication
was printed by
Beidel Printing House, Inc.
63 West Burd Street
Shippensburg, PA 17257-0708 USA

The acid-free paper used in this book meets the guidelines
for permanence and durability of the Committee on Production
Guidelines for Book Longevity of the Council on Library Resources.

For a complete list of available publications
please write
White Mane Books
Division of White Mane Publishing Company, Inc.
P.O. Box 708
Shippensburg, PA 17257-0708 USA

Library of Congress Cataloging-in-Publication Data

Kay, Alan N., 1965-
    Off to fight : young heroes of history / by Alan N. Kay.
      p. cm.
    Includes bibliographical references.
    Summary: Just when twelve-year-old George Adams has begun to settle into life in
Richmond, Virginia secedes from the Union, and George joins the boys he has become
friends with when they enlist to fight for the Confederacy.
    ISBN 1-57249-240-6 (alk. paper)
    1. Virginia--History--Civil War, 1861-1865--Juvenile fiction. [1.
Virginia--History--Civil War, 1861-1865--Fiction. 2. United States--History--Civil War,
1861-1865--Fiction.] I. Title.

PZ7.K178 Of 2001
[Fic]--dc21

                                                        2001055913

PRINTED IN THE UNITED STATES OF AMERICA

This book is dedicated to the millions of uncounted and unknown victims of war.

Contents

CHARACTERS

George Adams—A 12-year-old boy living in Richmond, Virginia. Our main character.

Sean Adams—George's father

Sallie (Davis) Adams—George's stepmother

Eric—A red-headed boy from Richmond who becomes George's best friend

Bobby—The leader of a gang in Richmond that George joins

John Webb—A slave friend of George's who works for his father

Allison Abigail Lancaster—A 9-year-old girl living in Fredericksburg, Virginia.

Confederate Commanders

General Robert E. Lee—Commander of the Army of Northern Virginia

General James Longstreet—General Lee's friend and a commander in his army

General George E. Pickett—A commander under Longstreet's command

Places

Richmond, Virginia—The capital of Virginia. It became the capital of the Confederacy during the Civil War.

Tredegar Iron Works—A factory in Richmond where
  George's father works
Fredericksburg, Virginia—A city caught between the
  Union army and the Confederate army.

PREFACE

WHAT IS HISTORICAL FICTION AND WHO ARE THE *YOUNG HEROES OF HISTORY*?

Young Heroes of History focuses on children and young adults who were heroes in their time. Although they may not have achieved fame or fortune, they made a difference in the lives of those near to them. Many were strong in body and spirit, but others managed to do the best they could in the time and place in which they lived.

Although the heroes of this series are fictional, these young Americans are placed in situations that were very real. The events of the time period as well as many of the people in these stories are accurately based on the historical records. Sometimes the language and actions of the people may be hard to understand or may seem inappropriate, but this was a different time.

Introduction

George loved Virginia. He had ever since he first set eyes on it. Its wide open spaces and lush green trees were so different from the cramped, dark place where he had lived in the North.

Richmond was his home now and he was never going back. Of course he remembered his days in Boston with his cousins and uncles, but ever since the John Brown incident, there had been a split in the family that seemed to be irreparable.

George had been at Harpers Ferry. He had seen John Brown and his followers try to take over the town and start a slave rebellion to free the slaves. He had even been held hostage by Brown for several days as he waited for the Marines to come to the rescue.[1] To George, John Brown was the most evil, horrid monster he could ever imagine.

George stayed and watched the trial. He listened as people argued and he sat spellbound as people defended this man as if he was some kind of saint. Throughout the North, certain people were claiming that Brown was doing what needed to be done. George couldn't believe what he was hearing.

---

1. You can read all about George and his Cousin David's adventure with John Brown in book two, of the Young Heroes of History Series, *On the Trail of John Brown's Body*.

What made matters even worse was that George's abolitionist cousins agreed with these people and thought that John Brown was a hero. They thought that a slave rebellion that killed thousands of Southerners and freed the slaves was a good thing. George couldn't understand their obsession with freeing the slaves. He was tired of their speeches and their secret meetings and their attitudes. All he wanted was to have fun and be a kid.

It was tough at first, leaving his large family and moving to a new city with just his dad. But after a few months they learned the ins and outs of the capital and were on their way to a fresh start. If only George could find some friends.

He never imagined a war would come. He never imagined that he would be one of the first to lie about his age and volunteer in that war. Sure he had always thought that being a soldier was a glorious adventure. He even thought it sounded like fun. He just never expected it to change his life forever.

GAMBLES HILL IN RICHMOND

Chapter One
Rock Fight

George looked at the line of hats on the ground. The game appeared to be easy enough: just hop over the hats, wave your arms, and everybody laughs. All of these other boys were able to do it just fine, and if George wanted them to be his friends, then he'd have to do it too.

"C'mon, new boy," the biggest boy teased. "We haven't got all day!"

George looked up again at the boys. About 12 of them were out today and all of them seemed to be waiting for him. He still didn't know many of their names, but he knew the name of their gang: Gambles Hill Cats.

What a great name! George had thought to himself when he and his dad had moved into their new house. It had seemed that every neighborhood in Richmond had some kind of gang, but George had never lived in any one spot in the city long enough to join one. Now that his dad had remarried and had found himself a steady job they finally were settled enough for George to try to join a gang.

The gangs were almost always divided into neighborhoods. George's new place on Byrd Street was near an empty hill that overlooked the James River. It had a spectacular view of the whole city and there was enough space on the hill to play games, war, chase, or anything else the boys wanted to do. Its height and steepness also made it the perfect location for a gang headquarters. With all that in mind, it was easy to name the gang after the hill where they played.

It had taken George several days to get the courage to approach the boys. They acted very secretive and suspicious of anybody who was not in their gang. At first, they chased him down the street until he ran back into his house. But George didn't give up. He knew if he ever wanted to have friends and be safe from some of the other gangs nearby, he would have to join these boys sooner or later.

George nervously looked down at the ten hats. It should be easy enough to complete the game. He lifted one leg and prepared to hop.

"Hey, wait a minute," the biggest boy shouted again. "Don't the new boys have to do the slope?"

"Yeah, the slope!" the boys all yelled in agreement. "Make him do the slope!"

George looked around anxiously wondering what was going on. He put his leg back down and watched as the boys picked up the hats and laid them out again in a diagonal line going down the slope of the hill.

"Now give it a go, new boy," the leader yelled at George. "And don't mess up."

George gulped as he looked out over the new course and realized how difficult it would be to hop over the hats and not lose his balance. The hats, only about three feet apart, were spread out on the steepest part of the hill. He knew that as he jumped he would be pulled down the hill faster and faster and it would be almost impossible to keep control of his momentum. But he had to do it! If he didn't, they'd never let him in the gang. But then again if he messed up, they might not let him in either.

Oh God, George prayed to himself, *help me not to mess up.*

George lifted his left leg and hopped over the first hat easily. The boys all laughed and cheered. A few of them yelled, "Go, boy, go!" while two or three yelled, "Fall! Fall!"

George, waving his arms as he had seen the other boys do, hopped over the second hat. It was easier than he thought. The next two hats also were simple, but then the slope of the hill got worse and George had to steady himself quickly with his arms. His speed picked up as he went farther down the hill, almost falling forward over the fourth hat.

"Roll! Roll!" the boys yelled. "He's gonna roll!"

George was almost out of control now. His arms were flailing everywhere, and the hill was pulling him faster and faster towards the bottom. He managed to hop over the next three hats, but now he was going so fast he couldn't stop. At the next hat, George hopped, cleared the hat, and landed awkwardly. Losing his balance, he rolled onto the grass all the way down to the bottom of the hill, flattening the remaining hats with his body as he went. The boys all laughed and cheered. Some of them danced around and a few of them slapped hands together.

George lay facedown on the grass listening to the laughter and feeling totally depressed and defeated, thinking he would never have any friends.

"The line, the line," the boys were yelling from the top of the hill.

George looked up to see the boys forming two lines, one next to the other. He took a deep breath and forced down any tears that might have been coming.

"C'mon, new boy," the leader shouted from the top. "It's time for you to crawl the line."

Crawl the line? George wondered to himself. *What was he talking about?*

George got up slowly and climbed to the top of the hill.

"Crawl through here," the leader said as he pointed to the two lines the boys had made. Each of them was standing with their hands in the air, grasping the hands of the boy across from them to make a small human tunnel. George prepared to crawl on his hands and knees through it quickly when the leader stopped him with his hand.

"Not so fast," he said. "You've got to go through the tunnel slow enough, so everyone gets their turn. Understand?"

George nodded to the boy as he thought to himself, *Gets their turn? Gets their turn at what?*

"This is your last chance," the leader warned him. "You've already messed up the hats. If you don't do this right, it's over."

George gulped again taking one last look at the boys. If he ever wanted a chance to join the gang it was now or never.

"New boy! New boy!" they chanted as George began to crawl.

As George approached the first pair of boys, they gave him a stinging spanking on his bottom and laughed gleefully. George let out a loud yell in surprise. The spankings really hurt. The boys gave him another spanking before he was out of reach. George let out another yell as tears began to form in his eyes.

Stop it! George shouted to himself. *You've got to do this or you'll be alone forever.*

George took a deep breath and began too crawl again. The spankings still stung but this time he was prepared for it. By the time George had neared the end of the human tunnel, he even slowed down to show the boys his toughness. Finally, the chantings and laughing had stopped, and the spankings had gotten a little weaker.

"Congratulations, you made it," the leader said as he greeted George at the end of the tunnel.

George let out a sigh of relief as he reached up to grab the leader's extended hand.

"Not bad for a first timer," the leader said as he pulled George up to his feet. "I didn't think you had it in you. The last kid to do it had to try three times before he had the guts to slow down."

"No big deal," George bragged. "I've been hit lots of times by my old man, my uncles, and even my older cousins. This wasn't much different."

"What's your name?" the boy asked.

"George...George Adams," he answered. "My dad and I just moved into the neighborhood last week."

"Where you from?" another of the boys asked as he walked toward George. "You don't sound like you're from Richmond."

"Ah...well, we just came from Kansas a year or two ago," George answered slowly. He did not want to tell the boys that he grew up in Boston. Northerners weren't too well liked right now, especially with the recent election of Abraham Lincoln to the presidency.

"You don't sound like you're from Kansas," another boy added.

"Well, actually I'm Irish," George answered truthfully. He *was* Irish after all and since he had lived in an Irish slum his accent sounded more Irish than Boston anyway.

"Hey, Bobby, are we gonna let him join or what?" one of the boys asked. Bobby, the tallest and biggest boy by far, was obviously the leader of the gang.

"Sure, why not?" Bobby answered. "We can always use more guys in the gang, especially ones who can take a little punishment."

"Hey, George," Bobby said, turning back again. "You ever been in any scrapes?"

"Sure have!" George said proudly. "My cousin and I used to fight with a gang back home all the time. I even got in a bar fight one time when my dad had an argument with his friends at a pub."

"Well, that's good," Bobby said quickly, ignoring George's excitement and continuing on, "cuz you're sure to see some fights with us."

"Sounds fine," George said quickly. He was looking forward to getting involved in some rough stuff. After all, his previous fights had been fun even though he got banged up a few times. He especially remembered the fight in the park in Boston when he tackled a boy twice his size and saved his cousin from a real beating. It was a thrill and well worth the few aches and pains he had afterwards. Still, looking up at his new friends, George couldn't help but feel a little nervous wondering how big these fights might be.

"Hey, Russell," Bobby called, turning to a small, fat boy with glasses, "tell George here the rules."

Russell walked toward George, took a deep breath, and stood directly in front of him. His eyes focused on George's face with an intensity that would have made George really nervous if Russell had not been so short. It was clear that he took his job seriously, but George could not help but smile as the strange little boy puffed out his chest and began to speak.

"First, you got to memorize the members' names and addresses," Russell began in a squeaky voice. He pointed to each boy as he told George the name and the exact place where they lived. George thought it a little strange that Russell took the time to not only give the address of each boy, but to also describe the house in minute detail. George listened intently, however, if for no other reason than when each boy's name was called they would stare at George to see whether he was paying attention.

"You got all that?" Russell asked when he was finished.

George took a few seconds to look over the gang. On his left was Bobby, the leader, Bruce with the blond hair, Eric with the red hair, Steven, Jason, and Peter.

On his right stood his next door neighbor Mike, Mike's Cousin Fred, little Jeremy, John, and another Peter. In front of him, of course, was Russell.

"Yeah, sure, I got all that," George said quickly. Everyone lived so close that he already knew where all of their houses were, so it would be a cinch to remember everything.

"Good," Russell continued. "Now as for the rules of the gang—"

"Hey, Bobby, do we gotta do this now?" the boy to George's left asked. "You know Russell is gonna take all day as he always does. Let's go have some fun."

"Yeah, alright Bruce," Bobby agreed as he turned towards Russell. "Why don't you finish this at your house later, Russell. That way you can take all the time you need."

"Well, O.K.," Russell said slowly with disappointment.

George wondered whether this was the only time anyone paid any attention to Russell.

"Whatcha got in mind, Bruce?" Bobby said, turning his attention away from Russell and George.

"Let's go get some candy over on Fifth Street," Bruce answered. "I got me a few cents and I'll share it with y'all."

"But what if the Fifth Street Cats are out?" another boy asked.

That's Fred, George reminded himself.

"Don't worry about them, Fred," Bruce answered. "Now that we got George here, we'll have more guys today than they do. Besides, they won't even see us."

George shifted nervously, feeling the added pressure from Bruce's comment.

"And if they do," Bobby added confidently, "we've got our little surprise all ready for them. Don't we, boys?"

"Sure do," several of the boys quickly shouted.

"Well then, let's go get some candy!" Bobby yelled.

"Yay!" the gang cheered.

The walk through the streets was a pleasant one. It was a warm spring day in Richmond, the kind which George loved the most. Winter had pretty much passed, yet there was still a crispness in the air that tickled the nose on occasion. The clear blue sky and bright sunlight made up for the lack of green leaves on the trees.

The gang walked quickly from street to street. At first, they were in their own territory so everyone was comfortable and playful. They made jokes, jumped around, scared a cat away, yelled at a dog, called to the young kids playing in the street, and even threw a couple of harmless pebbles at someone's window. But as they ventured from Fourth Street and headed towards the Fifth Street markets, their playfulness disappeared and the boys became quiet and nervous.

"Keep your eyes open," Bobby reminded them. "Our defense plan won't work if we get taken by surprise."

"Defense plan?" George repeated.

"Yeah," red-headed Eric answered, "we got this great plan if other gangs attack us."

"What is it?"

"It's real simple," Eric began. "Bobby and Bruce thought of it. All we got to do—"

"Hey, there's the store," Bruce called out.

"Oh boy," Eric said, "I think I'm gonna get me one of those chocolate things."

"I'm gonna get a popcorn ball," Russell said.

"I'm gonna get some taffy."

"Hey, hey," Bruce interrupted, "I don't have that much money."

The boys stopped talking and looked around quietly.

"I got a few cents too," George added quickly. No one noticed the nervousness in his voice. He was supposed to buy a loaf of bread for dinner with that money, but he knew this was a good chance to get popular with the guys.

"Hey all right, new guy," Bobby said smiling as he slapped George on the back. "You just might make a good Cat after all."

George smiled back as he stumbled forward a little from the force of Bobby's slap. The others laughed. George laughed too. In fact, he couldn't remember the last time he laughed and hung out with a group of kids. *This sure was fun,* he thought to himself.

The candy store was deserted except for a little kid buying some peanut brittle. Bobby reminded everyone to be well behaved; otherwise, the word would get out and they wouldn't be able to come there anymore. Besides, if they made too much noise the Fifth Street Cats might notice and ambush them.

The owner of the shop finished helping the little boy and turned his attention to the gang. He looked them over suspiciously, frowned a little, and walked to the counter nearest them.

"You boys got money?" he asked gruffly.

"Sure do," George piped in as he laid his coins on the table.

"Me too," Bruce added quickly.

"Well," the man said smiling, "glad to hear it. I've become pretty tired of boys coming in here, staring at my candy, and not buying anything. Just take your time and look around, boys, but don't touch nothing. You touch it, you buy it."

The boys spread out as they stared at the different candies, cookies, and baked goods. There even was a little ice cream in the corner sitting atop huge blocks of ice. George headed right for it knowing he might not get another chance to buy ice cream for awhile.

In the winter, ice was shipped from the frozen Northern lakes to the Southern states, but once summer arrived, ice cream was much harder to find.

"Excuse me," George said as he brushed past the little boy. The boy stared strangely at George. Then he slowly went outside where he continued to watch the boys through the window.

"Hey, Eric," George said slowly, "you see that little kid?"

"Yeah, so?" Eric said.

"He's staring at us awful strangely," George replied.

"Don't worry about it," Eric answered. "Let's get some candy before we got to leave."

"Yeah, O.K.," George said slowly as he turned his head away from the boy. As he did so, the boy suddenly turned and ran across the street.

It only took a few minutes for everyone to get what they wanted and to pay the owner. George waited patiently eating his ice cream while the man counted all the money.

"Thanks a lot, boys. And come back again sometime!"

"We will," Mike and Peter answered as the boys walked out of the store. They stepped out onto the street and began to walk back towards home. Each boy was sucking on a candy or chewing on a cookie or licking his ice cream while they stared at one another's food. Before too long they had traded bites or licks or even the whole candy, often not paying attention to where they were going.

"Going somewhere?" a voice suddenly said.

The boys looked up to see a group of approximately 10 boys standing with their arms crossed directly in their path. It was the Fifth Street Cats. Standing in front of them was the little boy from the candy shop.

Oh crud, George said to himself. *I knew we should've watched that kid.*

"As a matter of fact we are going somewhere," Bobby said quickly and boldly.

"It better be back to your territory," the leader of the other gang said.

"And what if it's not?" Bobby challenged.

"Then we'll take you there ourselves."

"You just try," Bruce shouted back.

"Why you little," the leader growled. "Get 'em, Cats!"

"Yaaahhhh!" the Fifth Street Cats yelled as they jumped at George and his friends.

"To the hill!" shouted Bobby as he turned and ran. The other boys turned around and followed Bobby. George, however, was caught more by surprise and stood for an extra second.

Two Fifth Streeters headed right for him. George jumped back, threw his ice cream in the first boy's face, turned, and ran as well.

"Yukkkk!" the boy yelled as the ice cream hit him in the eye. "Come back here, you little jerk!"

George laughed as he caught up with the rest of the gang.

"Where are we headed, Eric?" he said between breaths.

"To the hill, dummy," Eric answered.

"What for?" George cried.

"To carry out Bobby's plan," Eric shouted. "Don't you remember?"

"No!" George yelled back as he sidestepped one of the Fifth Streeters, who had managed to catch up. "You never told me!"

"Well, just follow me!" Eric yelled as he ran faster to escape.

The boys took a sharp left and a hard right turn to get away from the gang immediately behind them. George could run faster than many of his friends, but he had to follow them because he was unsure of the new neighborhood streets.

"Gotcha," one of the Fifth Streeters cried as he grabbed George's arm.

"George," Eric yelled as he looked back and saw George beginning to be surrounded.

"Bobby!" Eric called ahead. "The new guy has been caught."

Bobby slowed down obviously thinking about turning around while Russell shouted: "C'mon...c'mon, we gotta keep going."

But then with a sudden burst of energy, George whipped around, punched the Fifth Streeter in the nose, and broke free of his grip.

"Yeah, George!" Eric called as George began to run again.

"My nose!" the Fifth Streeter cried as his hands covered his bloody face.

"Yaahhhhh!" the Fifth Streeters yelled again, this time with anger and hatred in their voices. "Get them!"

"Go! Go! Go!" George shouted at the rest of the gang, who had slowed down to watch. He was running so fast, he almost overtook Bobby and even Russell, who had never even stopped.

"This way, this way," Bobby called to George as they approached another corner.

"Nice shot, George," Bobby said as he and George ran side by side.

"Thanks," George said proudly. *That punch did more to impress his new friends than anything else,* George thought to himself.

"Just better hope they don't catch us," Bobby continued, "or that kid will kill you."

George gulped as he looked at the hill coming into view.

"There it is," Bobby yelled. "Everyone to your stations!"

The boys all scattered to different points on the hill while George tried to decide what to do. He looked behind him to catch sight of the Fifth Streeters making their way up the hill. Bobby and Bruce headed straight up the hill while the others branched off to the left and right and moved into position behind different trees. George looked around again in confusion.

"George, over here," Eric called from behind his tree.

George turned and headed towards Eric. Nearing the tree, George felt a sudden pain in his shoulder that knocked him to the ground.

"Aaarrrgghh!" George screamed as he turned to look at what struck him. A rock whizzed past his head and he barely moved out of the way in time.

"Quick, George, before you get hit again," Eric called as he waved George to come over.

Despite the pain in his shoulder, George crawled on the grass towards the tree, keeping his head down to avoid the rush of rocks.

"What's going on?" George cried as he made it to safety.

"Rock fight," Eric answered simply, his red hair blowing in the breeze and his face hidden behind a tree branch. "Ain't you ever been in one?"

"No," George replied.

"Well, just grab some rocks and get ready," Eric said, never taking his eyes off the fight.

"Get ready for what?"

"The signal, dummy," Eric answered quickly. He was obviously annoyed that George never knew the plan even though Eric forgot to tell him. "You think we ran all the way here just to hide behind the trees? Bobby wanted to lure them here, so we could ambush them."

"Great!" George replied as a rock hit the tree and bounced away.

"See these rocks at my feet?" Eric continued. "We put them here a week ago when Bobby thought of the plan. Then we got rid of all the rocks in the middle of the hill. As soon as they are within range, we will let our rocks fly and they will have no ammunition to throw back at us. It will be a slaughter!"

George looked down at the advancing Fifth Streeters while Eric smiled gleefully. It was almost time. George picked up some rocks.

Di-de-di-di-di-de-di-de-deee, the sound of a bugle suddenly blurted out.

"The signal!" Eric cried. "Do it!"

All the boys in George's gang suddenly threw rock after rock after rock at the Fifth Street Cats. It was as if the clouds suddenly opened up and rained rocks down on the boys. They were hit in the head, in the face, and in the arms and the legs. They started to bleed and scream as the rocks bruised their bones and opened cuts in their skin. Trying to dodge the rocks they ducked their heads and covered them with their arms. They screamed and cried and ran.

"Hah-hah!" Eric yelled. "They're dropping like flies!"

"Don't let up!" George heard Bobby call. "Some of 'em are still standing their ground."

George threw his rocks hitting one of the boys still standing. He fell to the ground.

"Good throw, George," Bruce shouted from across the hill.

George turned and looked up the hill. A rock smashed him suddenly in the face. Peter, who was at the tree nearest George, threw another rock at George's attacker and knocked him down as well. Then he ran to George lying on the ground.

"George...George, you alright?" Peter called as he lifted George's bloody face off the grass. Blood covered the grass and George's eyes were half-open.

"Cover them, boys!" Bobby yelled as the boys threw more rocks at the few Fifth Street Cats who remained. The rock throwing lasted only another few seconds when the last of the Fifth Streeters gave up and ran away.

"Yaaayy!" Eric, Bruce, and the others cried when the last of them turned tail and ran. "We won!"

"Peter, how's the new guy?" Bobby immediately called out.

"He's just coming around," Peter answered. "I think his jaw is broken."

"Ooohhhh," George groaned. "Wha happah?"

"Don't talk, George," Bobby said as he kneeled on the grass next to George. "You got a bad hit in the face and it's probably gonna swell up real nice. You did good, new guy, real good."

"Fanks," George mumbled as he gently touched his face. "Ooohhh gosh. Dish weally hurts."

"Hey, don't worry about it," Eric said as he walked toward George. "You got yourself a real live battle wound. I bet your dad's gonna be real proud of you."

"My dad," George moaned. "Oh God, what am I gonna tell my dad?"

CHAPTER TWO

EGGS

"Oh, George," his stepmother, Sallie, said softly. "What am I going to do with you?"

George didn't answer. He couldn't. His stepmother was holding his jaw tightly as she cleaned off the new blood that had soaked through the bandages. Fortunately, the jaw was not broken, but the moment that George had returned home from the fight, his stepmother had wrapped the jaw so tight that he could barely chew his food.

"Ow!" George cried pulling his head away. It had been two days since his injury and his face still was extremely sensitive. The large black bruise on his left cheek, where the rock had hit him, had swollen so much that it looked as if George was hiding a baseball in his mouth. Even talking hurt.

"Stay still," his stepmother barked sharply. "How can I clean you up if you keep moving?"

"It hurts," George mumbled.

"Of course it does," his stepmother said spitefully. "You're lucky you didn't break it, you and your stupid gang fights."

George ignored her comment. He just stared off into space. He didn't want to listen to another speech about the evils of gangs. She thought gangs were for lower-class boys, not for someone like George who someday, she hoped, would become a gentleman.

Gentleman, George had laughed, as if he wanted to be one of those snobby, stuck-up guys riding in their carriages and talking all day. *Besides, their kids joined gangs too, so what was the big deal?*

"There, you're all set," his stepmother said when the bandages were wrapped in place. "Now, go back to your room until your father gets home. I have to take the twins out for the day."

"Yes ma'am," George mumbled as he slowly went to his room.

This, being grounded, stinks, he thought to himself as he jumped on the bed and listened to his stepmother getting ready to leave. He heard the noisy clatter of dishes and the whining of his stepbrother and sister. He could care less about them right now. All he cared about was being with his friends. He buried his head into his pillow and closed his eyes.

Tap, tap, tap.

George stirred in his bed.

Tap, tap, tap.

George opened his eyes. He must have drifted off to sleep. Someone was banging on his window.

George sprang off his bed and walked towards the noise.

"Who's there?" he whispered as he opened the window and slowly poked his head outside.

"It's me, Eric," said a voice from the street.

"Eric?" George repeated. "What are you doing here?"

"I came to get you," Eric whispered as he approached the window. "But your mom told me you couldn't come out."

"She ain't my mom," George said quickly and bitterly. "She's my stepmom."

"Oh, whatever," Eric said. "Why can't you come out?"

"I've been grounded," George said angrily.

"Grounded?" Eric repeated. "For what?"

"For getting into a fight," George replied. "And for using my bread money to buy you guys candy."

"That was your bread money?" Eric said in surprise.

"Yeah," George said slowly.

"Wow," Eric said softly as his head fell back a little and he began to think about what a neat thing George had done.

"And, your stepmom grounded you for that?" Eric continued after a few moments of silence.

"No, my dad did."

"I thought you said your dad was your friend," Eric said with a look of confusion on his face. Even though he had only spent a short time with George at the candy shop he could already tell how much George cared for his father.

"He is," George said in a frustrated voice. "But he always does what my stepmom wants now. He used to think our fighting was kind of funny. He didn't even want to punish me until Sallie opened her mouth."

"How long are you grounded?" Eric asked.

"Two weeks," George mumbled.

"Two weeks for that?" Eric repeated.

"Yeah," George complained. "But I think it's just 'cause she wants me to do chores. All day long I've been cleaning up the house, watching her kids, cleaning the cupboards, and anything else that woman wants me to do."

"That stinks," Eric said.

"I know," George agreed. "But what can I do?"

"You can sneak out," Eric suggested quickly.

"No way," George answered. "I'm not gonna get in more trouble."

"Well, O.K.," Eric said teasingly. "But you're gonna miss all the fun."

"What fun?"

"Bobby wants to throw eggs at the convention," Eric answered.

"Throw eggs at the convention?" George repeated.

"Yeah, you know," Eric answered, "that convention discussing whether Virginia should leave the Union or not. Bobby's dad has been complaining about them from the day they first met. He thinks that they are all a bunch of cowards."

"They are," George said quickly. "All they ever do is talk and talk."

"I know," Eric agreed. "That's why Bobby wants to throw eggs at some of the ones who want to talk to Lincoln and be all nice and all. Bobby's dad says we should join South Carolina and the others and quit the Union now while we can."

"So who's Bobby gonna pelt?" George asked.

"I'm not sure," Eric replied with a shrug of his shoulders. "He's got a whole bunch of rotten eggs that he's been saving for just such an occasion."

"Oh, that sounds like fun," George whined.

"Why don't you come?" Eric suggested again. "Your stepmom will be gone for a while, won't she?"

"Yeah," George said slowly.

"And your dad works all day, right?"

"Yeah,"

"Well then, what are you waiting for?" Eric shouted happily. "C'mon!"

George looked back into the empty house, shrugged his shoulders, and climbed out the window. He hated sneaking out even if no one would know. It wasn't because he was afraid of getting caught. There wasn't much else his parents could do to him anyway. It wasn't because he was concerned about his stepmother. She'd never liked him from the first day they met. It was mainly because he hated to deceive his dad. Even if the punishment was made up by his stepmom, his dad agreed to it and would be angry with George; but he also couldn't pass up this chance to get more chummy with the gang. If they thought he was afraid, he'd never have any friends. Besides, this sounded like fun!

Eric led George to the hill where the others were waiting.

"Hey, George," Bruce called when he saw them coming. "How's the jaw?"

"O.K.," George said. "It ain't broke, just really sore."

"That's good," Bruce answered. "We were afraid that you broke it or something and wouldn't be able to join us."

"You kidding?" George quickly bragged. "I wouldn't miss this for the world!"

"Good," Bobby joined in. "You're the last one here, so we can get going. The convention will let out soon, so we gotta hurry."

"You sure you wanna do this, Bobby?" Russell suddenly interrupted. "I mean, a lot of people in Richmond don't agree with your dad. They think we should stay in the Union."

"They're all a buncha cowards!" Bobby shouted. "They think that we can sit back and watch as them Northerners get their way in everything."

Russell stared at Bobby in confusion.

"That Lincoln guy is all for the North," Bobby tried to explain. "Not one Southern state voted for him and especially not Virginia. Now, we got us a president who hates slavery and is gonna tell us to free all our slaves as soon as he gets the chance."

"He ain't gonna make us free our slaves," Peter interrupted. He had been listening to the argument and didn't really care much for either Russell or Bobby. It bothered him that Bobby made it sound so simple. "Lincoln may not like slavery but he just doesn't want it to grow. Besides, how can he free our slaves when the rest of the government don't want him to?"

"It ain't just Lincoln," Bobby almost yelled. "It's all them Northerners who want our slaves freed."

"C'mon, Bobby," Peter said doubtfully.

"No, you c'mon," Bobby said angrily. "Don't you remember John Brown? Heck, it was only two years ago when he tried to lead a slave revolt against all of us right here in Virginia!"

"I remember John Brown," George interrupted suddenly. "I was there with him when he tried it."

The boys stared blankly at George. What was he talking about?

"No, really," George said quickly. It was obvious the gang thought he was crazy. "I was really there, at Harpers Ferry, the night that Brown carried out his raid."

"Why were you there?" Peter said doubtfully.

"My dad and I had heard about the plan when we were in Kansas, and we were on our way to stop him when we got caught," George said quickly.

"If you were with John Brown that night," Russell said smartly, "then what did he steal from Colonel Washington, hhhmmmm?"

"He stole George Washington's sword, of course," George quickly answered.

The gang looked at George and Russell. George was right.

"Listen, I was there," George continued quickly before anyone else could interrupt him. "And I'm telling you that Bobby is right. Some of them Northerners are crazy. Not crazy like Brown was, but crazy enough to think that a slave rebellion was a good thing."

"What are you talking about?" Peter said softly.

"What I'm telling you is that the whole time Brown was on trial and even afterwards, lots of people from the North were saying that Brown was right, for slavery was evil and that the South deserved what was coming and all that other stuff!"

"You see," Bobby quickly added. "I am right. Them Northerners hate us and look down on us and as soon as they get their chance they are gonna start telling us what we can and cannot do. Now who's with me for some good ol' egg throwing?"

"I am!" George said first.

"Me too," added Eric and Bruce.

The other boys joined in, even Russell and Peter. After the eggs were handed out, the boys made their way downtown.

It didn't take long to reach the capital area. A few detours were taken to avoid the Fifth Street Cats' territory because Bobby wasn't in the mood for another fight today.

As usual, the capital square was quite busy with the crowds of people attending the convention. In addition there was the usual people conducting governmental business at the state court, the post office, and the governor's house. People also were checking in and out of hotels scattered around the outskirts of the square and were visiting banks and shops that opened their doors to the public.

Some people gathered outside the convention building to discuss political issues or just waited for a chance to talk with one of the governmental officials attending the convention. Bobby instructed the gang to scatter amongst the crowd and to make sure that no police officers were near them when the convention ended.

"Remember, the guy we're looking for is a real fatso," Bobby whispered to the boys.

"You mean the lawyer guy?" Peter asked.

"They're all lawyers," Russell added.

"Marmaduke Johnson is his name," Bobby said impatiently. "You know him. He's the guy who the newspapers are always poking fun at."

"Yeah," Eric agreed. "My dad's been reading about him in the *Examiner*. He thinks there's gonna be a duel between Johnson and the newspaper editor if things don't change soon."

"Well, there's gonna be some action right now," Bobby said with a grin. "Remember, do not throw the eggs until you hear my signal. Then let 'er rip and run straight for the river. We'll meet back at the hill when it's all over. Understand?"

"Yeah," several of the boys said grinning as they nodded there heads. "We understand. This is gonna be great."

The boys spread out in several directions looking for a good spot to see the doors. George found a place with Eric that provided a clear shot at the steps leading out of the building. The two of them stood with their hands in their pockets, nervously gripping the eggs and trying to look as natural as possible.

On the other side of the steps George could see Russell and Peter. Everyone else seemed to be outside of George's line of vision, but he knew that Bobby and Bruce were probably together as close to the front as possible. The doors began to open.

"Here they come," Eric whispered excitedly to George as he readied the three eggs he had taken out of his pockets.

Slowly, the men began to file out of the building and down the steps, two or three at a time. After 5 minutes had passed and over 20 men had made their way out, George began to wonder whether Johnson was even there today.

"Where is he?" Eric wondered out loud.

"I don't know," George answered.

"Maybe he ain't here today," Eric guessed.

"Can you see Bobby?" George asked.

"No, but I can see Russell," Eric replied.

"What's he doing?"

"He's looking away," Eric answered. "I think he and Peter are gonna give up."

"Those babies," George complained. "Can't they wait just a little longer?"

"Maybe we should try to find Bobby," Eric suggested.

"Yeah, O.K.," George agreed, turning his back towards the building and looking at the crowd.

Eric grabbed George's shoulder and tugged.

"There he is!" Eric shouted.

George turned and saw a well-dressed and very large rotund man walking out the door and into the late day sun. He was reading some papers as he walked and was not paying any attention to the discussions around him.

A high-pitched chirp, like the sound of a crow, pierced the air around them.

"The signal!" George cried.

Suddenly, from every direction, small eggs came flying through the air towards the fat man on the stairs. Some landed harmlessly on the ground near him, a few hit other men accidently, but most of them landed right on target.

"Aaahhhh!" the man screamed as smelly, old eggs struck him in the face, on the shoulders, and all over his large belly.

George laughed uncontrollably as threw his own eggs and watched as they knocked the papers from the man's hands and splattered his eyes.

"What the...stop!...no!" the man yelled.

The eggs kept coming from every direction. By the time George and Eric had thrown all of their eggs, the man was covered from head to toe with smelly, dripping yolks and discolored egg whites.

Laughter erupted from the boys as well as from the crowd.

"Serves you right!" one of the adults in the crowd yelled.

The man looked at the crowd trying to determine who had thrown the eggs. Grabbing a handkerchief from his pocket, he began wiping his face and clothes. Jokes and laughter echoed through the crowd until the man spotted a police officer nearby.

"Officer!" the man yelled, pointing in George's direction. "Arrest these young upstarts!"

George turned and saw the police officer running towards them.

"Let's get out of here!" he yelled to Eric.

Eric and George sprinted out of the courtyard and headed towards the streets. The other boys ran in the same direction as the police officer followed.

"Stop right there!" the policeman yelled in vain.

Bobby and Bruce came up behind Eric and George as they rounded a corner.

"Hah, hah!" Bobby laughed. "Did you see the look on Johnson's face when I hit him in the nose?"

"Yeah," Eric answered. "He looked mad enough to eat nails!"

"This was a great idea, Bobby," George said as he continued to run alongside of him. He really meant it to. It felt great being part of a group again and having people to laugh and hang out with. Even though they were running from a police officer and in danger of being thrown in jail, he couldn't help but feel warm and comfortable inside. Finally, he had friends again.

"Hold it right there!" another policeman shouted as he appeared directly in front of the four boys.

"This way!" Bobby shouted as he turned into an alley.

The boys ran behind Bobby as the second policeman was joined by the one from the capital.

"What do we do, Bobby?" Eric cried. "We're heading away from the river."

"I don't know yet," Bobby answered quickly. "Maybe we should split up."

"Going somewhere, boys?" a voice said in front of them.

Eric, George, Bobby, and Bruce stopped dead in their tracks and stared at the group of boys blocking their path. It was the Fifth Street Cats.

"Oh no," George moaned.

"We're doomed," Eric cried in despair.

"Look, Cats," Bobby began quickly, still panting from the chase. "We ain't got time for this now. We're being followed by the police cuz we—"

"We know exactly what you did," the leader interrupted, "and we thought it was great."

The four boys looked at each other in confusion.

"And despite what you did the other day," he continued, "we're gonna help you."

"Gee thanks, Kevin," Bobby said to the leader. He had known Kevin for a long time and had never known him to do anything nice. As gang leaders the two had butted heads regularly, which made this act of kindness all the more strange.

"Don't get the wrong idea," Kevin said quickly. "We still owe you guys big, but we don't like that lawyer any more than you do. Sooner or later Virginia is gonna leave the Union and join the other Southern states. That old man and others like him are only holding the South back. But there's no time for talk now. Hide in here."

"Thanks," the boys said as they ducked into the alley that Kevin had pointed to.

"Oh, and Bobby," Kevin warned him, "watch your back, cuz the next time we won't be friends."

The door slammed open, smashing into the wooden wall and startling everyone.

"By God they've done it!" George's father, Sean, cried.

George looked up in surprise to see the huge figure of his father partly rush then stagger into the room. He was wearing the same overalls he always wore and as usual, they were completely covered with dirt and soot. His father's red hair was standing up in every direction as if he had just walked through a tornado while his large hands were covered with dirt that only the whites of his knuckles shone through.

"Done what, dear?" George's stepmother, Sallie, asked. Her young voice and pretty face reminded George that she was still a young woman of 25 and closer to George's age than his father's. George was sure that her prettiness had led his father to remarry so quickly after their arrival in Richmond. It could only be that because George could find no other qualities worth admiring in his stepmother. In George's opinion, she was shallow, stupid, and selfish, and the only thing that kept George from running away was his respect and admiration for his father.

George knew that it had not been easy for his father to pick up and move to Richmond, Virginia. After the raid on Harpers Ferry, the death of George's Uncle John and Aunt Regina, and the disappearance of his cousin, David, George's father had decided to leave the North. He chose Richmond because it was a large enough city in which to find work fairly easily. Indeed, within two weeks of arriving, his father had landed a job at the Tredegar Iron Works. It was the largest industry of its kind in the South and it even owned slaves. Because he was fortunate enough to be able to read and write, George's father had rapidly advanced within the company. If only he hadn't fallen in love with Sallie, George and his father would still be best friends.

"The Carolinians have taken Fort Sumter," his father exclaimed as he paced around the room. "The Federals have surrendered!"

"Yee-haaa, that was quick!" George exclaimed, as he jumped out of his chair and held his fist in the air. He had been afraid that his father had found out about the egging and was relieved that his secret was still safe.

"Hallelujah!" Sallie joined in as she patted the baby in her lap. George had a 2-year-old stepbrother, Jerry, and stepsister, Martha, who were twins and always got him into trouble. Although they were cute and adorable, he had little love for them at times, especially on days like today when he was forced to stay home and help his stepmother take care of sick Martha.

"Now you two have gone and done it," George's father scolded. "You've upset little Martha again with your yelling. Look at her crying now. I just don't understand you. You're just like all the other crazies downtown with your hooting and hollering and carrying on. I can barely stand it. It's been going on all afternoon."

"Well, people are happy, Sean," Sallie answered back. "They're glad that something is finally going to happen."

"Well, they're keeping me from getting my work done," Sean said in an annoyed tone. "Everyday it's been one disturbance after another, but today has been the worst by far."

George and his stepmother sat quietly and waited for him to continue.

"There I was working in the factory," he began, "and normally it's so loud I can't hear nothing outside. Then around three o'clock there was such whooping and hollering both inside and outside that all of the men rushed outside to hear Smith's armory band play their bugles and snare drums. Then someone brought out a Confederate flag, while the band started playing "Dixie," and pretty soon everyone was hollering, dancing, and carrying on. There must have been thousands of people yelling for secession and independence. Oh, you should have heard it all!"

"Well a-l-l-right," George chimed in. "It's good to see we got so many patriotic Virginians. I thought we'd never have the guts to do anything except complain like those foolish politicians who've been arguing for months about what to do about Mr. Lincoln..."

"Those 'foolish politicians' as you call them," his father quickly interrupted, "seem to be the only ones with their heads on straight. They're not jumping the gun and following the South Carolinians just because it feels good. They're thinking about all the ways Virginia might be affected by this whole situation."

"But they've been talking forever," George complained. "What has it been, 2 or 3 months now since Lincoln was elected?"

"Almost 5. But listen, son, I know you and I don't agree on this whole secession thing. You've been hanging around with them kids who've been causing all that trouble."

George quickly looked up at his father and met his gaze. Did he know about the egg incident after all? His father smiled slightly as if he might know but wasn't about to say anything. At least his stepmother appeared to be completely unaware of the little secret between them.

"Now, don't get me wrong, son," his father continued once it was clear that George understood what he had hinted at. "I am glad to see that you've made some friends and finally started thinking of Virginia as your home. But, it upsets me to see you acting and yelling without thinking like the rest of them in that mob today."

"I am thinking, Pa," George shot back. "I'm thinking about our pride and honor. Why are we gonna let a man like Mr. Lincoln lead us and tell us what to do like we got no rights?"

"We ain't gonna let him lead us around, but we also aren't gonna let those South Carolinians lead us with their rebellious talk. They've had big mouths for years and years, son. Heck, before you were born they were complaining about the government and threatening to secede at every crisis. Now, when things are at their worst, they are making the most noise. But we can't listen without thinking. We've got to decide what is best for Virginia! Not for South Carolina or for Mr. Lincoln."

"Oh but, Sean," Sallie interrupted in a high-pitched voice. "Mr. Lincoln will lead us to ruin! He'll set free all of our slaves, destroy our plantations, and ruin our whole livelihood."

"Well that remains to be seen, dear. The man's just been elected and he's no devil as the Carolinians would like us to believe. Mind you, I don't agree with his ideas and I don't much like him, but I'm not gonna condemn a man without so much as a thought."

"Well, I am!" George shouted as he stood up to face his father. Even at 12 years old, George was still a full head shorter than his father. The mere act of craning his neck to look his father in the eyes was enough to let out some of the steam in his anger. "Lincoln is not our president! Not one Southern state voted for him. He's been an anti-slavery abolitionist for as long as I can remember, and all you and the rest of the politicians are doing by delaying us is making Virginia look weak!"

"Son," George's father began, placing his hand firmly yet gently on his son's shoulder, "as long as you can remember is only about 12 years. You're still young, still wet behind the ears. You've not seen how men can say one thing and mean another or change their opinions over the years or overnight. I know you've been hanging around with lots of others who are calling for secession but please, you've got to think!"

"I am thinking, Pa," George yelled, grabbing his father's hand and throwing it off his shoulder. He hated when his father talked to him like he was still just a kid or that he was stupid. "I'm thinking that you're a coward and the only reason you're saying this all to me is because you're afraid to fight!"

George stepped suddenly backwards in fear. What had he said? He didn't mean that. Why was everyone staring at him? He turned toward his father. Sean's teeth were clenched and his fists were shaking as if they were about to explode. His dark green eyes stared straight through George as if they could burn a hole into his head. George looked around the room nervously and fidgeted—even the babies were quiet. Noises of celebration could be heard from outside in the streets.

George knew that his father was trying to control his rage. He had never hit George. He had come close several times, like the time when George yelled at Sallie, but his father never really would have hit him over that. The two of them sometimes acted more like friends rather than father and son. It had been that

way ever since his mother died. When it was just the
two of them alone in Richmond, they spent all of their
time together. Laughing, joking, going out to the park,
cooking, and even working together. They were insepa-
rable. Even his father's second wife and children did
not come between the special relationship that George
had with his father.

George and his father used to be able to talk
about anything. They would sit under the stars of
the Kansas prairie and stay up all night discussing
family, girls, George's mother, and sometimes even
politics. What was happening? How had George let
this stupid discussion over rights and slavery come
between them? George had not meant to call his father a coward, he was only angry. His father was one
of the bravest men he'd ever known, but it was too
late to retract what he had already said. His words
had hurt his father—he could see the anger, sadness,
and loneliness that he had caused. Things would
never be the same again. Even if George apologized,
his father would always think that George did not
respect and look up to him. George felt like crying.
The whole thing seemed so stupid now, but what
could he do?

"I'm sorry you feel that way, son," his father finally said in almost a whisper. "And I don't know what
to say to change your mind. Why it's almost funny that
you say that since if there is a war, I won't be able to
fight anyway."

"You won't?" George gasped in amazement. Now
he was really confused.

"No, I won't. But not for the reason you accuse me
of. You see, son, if there is a war I will be one of the
first ones called upon. Not to fight, but to work. My job
here in the iron works is important now but will become even more important if war comes. They'll need
me to help the factory supply all of the guns and cannon that the South will need. And despite what you

TREDEGAR IRON WORKS IN RICHMOND, WHERE GEORGE'S FATHER WORKS

think, if that happens I will do it proudly because Virginia is my home now too and I will help to defend it in any way I can."

CHAPTER FOUR
THE CELEBRATION

A week later things were not any better between George and his father or the South and the North. President Lincoln had requested that Virginia send troops to help put down the rebellion in South Carolina. Virginia responded by seceding from the Union, causing the whole city of Richmond to become alive with the excitement of preparing for war. Bands played in the streets, speeches were made, flags flew, soldiers marched, and everywhere people went they did it with a new nervous energy and excitement.

The most remarkable event was the huge parade on the night of April 19. The city glowed with a brilliance of a million fireflies from lamps and lighted torches. Many buildings had their lamps turned on in the form of a cross; if the building did not have enough lights to form a cross then at least several lights glowed in the windows. Hundreds of people marched down Marshall Street carrying torches in their hands, and made their way towards the capital. Rockets flashed in all directions, Roman candles darted everywhere, bands played, and thousands of people sang along. By the time the parade reached the capital square, the streets were so full that the crowd could hardly move.[1]

---

1. This is how Sallie B. Putnam, a Richmond lady, described that day in her journal of 1861.

"Can you believe this?" Bobby said to George from their spot in front of the Exchange Hotel. "It's like nothing I've ever seen in my life."

"You'd never know that two weeks ago we were arguing with each other over whether to leave the Union," George agreed.

"It's like we're one big happy family," Bruce added.

"Sure is great," Russell commented.

"My fellow Virginians!" a voice shouted over the crowd from the hotel.

A few people in front quieted down, but for the most part, the crowd continued celebrating.

"My fellow Virginians!" the man repeated. This time he got the attention of most of the people within earshot. He paused while they looked towards him.

"Today is a great day," the man began. "For today we stand up for what we believe in!"

The crowd cheered. George, Bruce, Bobby, and the rest of the gang threw their fists in the air and cheered along with them.

"Today, we stand up for the South!"

More cheers.

"Today, we stand up for state's rights!"

More cheers.

"But most of all, today, we stand up for the Old Dominion! God bless Virginia!"

The crowd went wild with cheers, one of the bands began to play, and fireworks exploded into the night sky.

"This is incredible!" George shouted over the noise.

"Yeah," Bobby agreed. "I told you that once we left the Union we'd all stand together."

"I suppose you're right," Russell said.

"Of course I am," Bobby answered quickly. "I'm older than any of you and I know what this state is made of. Nobody pushes Virginia around."

"You tell 'em, Bobby," Bruce added. He was almost as old as Bobby and many of the boys considered him second in command of the gang. "You've always been right about that. The others were just...uh-oh."

"What?" Bobby asked, looking around.

"There's a policeman over there," Bruce answered. The boys all looked in the direction that Bruce had nodded.

"So?" Russell asked. "There are policemen everywhere."

"But that's the one who chased us the other day, remember?" Bruce pointed out.

"You think he recognizes us?" George asked.

"I don't know," Bobby answered. "But I'm not waiting around to find out. Let's move."

The boys made their way slowly through the crowd. The going was tough as they had to push through hundreds of people and constantly stop to apologize for bumping into a man or knocking into a lady. George was almost belted by an older gentleman when he accidentally knocked off his wife's hat. But the man let George pass when he saw that he was only a kid.

"Whew," Bobby said once they were out of the crowd. The noise of the bands and rockets was still loud enough that they had to shout to be heard. "I thought we'd never get out. Is everyone here?"

The boys all looked around, nodding their heads up and down and pointing at each other as they counted to see if they were all there.

"Looks like we're all here," Bruce answered.

"Good," Bobby said, looking around and trying to decide what to do next. "Let's find somewhere else to hang out."

The boys all turned down Main Street and headed towards the rear part of the parade. People were still crowding the streets as the noises of the bands and the cheering of the crowd continued to fill the night air.

"What do you think's gonna happen now?" Jason asked no one in particular. He had kept pretty quiet all night and in fact, George had hardly talked to him at all since he joined the gang. Once or twice he had tried to strike up a conversation, but Jason never seemed that interested in talking, as if it was uncomfortable for him.

"Don't know," Bruce said quickly.

"Think there will be a war?" Jason asked.

"Probably so," Bruce answered. "Lincoln's already calling for volunteers."

"I sure hope so," Bobby jumped in. "Then we can finally show the North what we Virginians are made of!"

"Yeah, we'll kick their butts," George added.

"Are you gonna sign up?" Jason asked Bobby in a soft voice.

"Huh?" Bobby said, caught off guard. "Me?"

"Yeah, you're old enough," Jason said. "My dad says that any boy who's old enough to hold a rifle can sign up."

"That ain't so," Bruce interrupted. "My dad's already in the militia and he told me that you have to be 18 to join."

"Officially maybe," Jason answered. "But you know that they'll take younger kids during a war. And even if they don't, you can always lie about your age. How are they gonna know?"

"Are you gonna sign up?" Russell asked Jason.

"Yeah," Jason answered with little emotion in his voice. "I have to. My dad got a bum leg from the Mexican War and he says that I have to keep the family tradition alive. He says that there's been a Ferguson in every war since the American Revolution."

"What about your brother?" Bobby asked. "Ain't he older than you?"

"Yeah," Jason answered. "He's gonna sign up too."

"Well heck," Bobby said suddenly. "We can't let you go all alone. We Cats stick together. Right, boys?"

"Right!" the boys shouted.

"And if Jason's gonna sign up, then we should too!" Bobby continued.

"Yeah!" Bruce shouted loudly, throwing his fist up in the air. "Let's do it!"

"Yeah!" Steven yelled too.

"Let's do it!" Jeremy hollered.

"But we might get killed!" Russell suddenly interrupted.

"So?" Bobby shouted back. "You afraid?"

"Yeah," Russell answered boldly. He might be the fall guy of the group, but he wasn't going to let Bobby bully him this time. "Who wouldn't be afraid? Only idiots don't think about that stuff."

"You calling me an idiot?" Bobby shot back.

"N-n-no," Russell answered nervously, taking a step backwards. "I simply meant that everyone is afraid of dying."

"Well, I'm not," Bobby said defiantly.

"Besides," Bruce quickly added, seeing that some of the boys were beginning to listen to Russell and not to Bobby. "We ain't gonna die. Them Northerners have no idea how to fight. Heck, the war will probably be over before we even get there."

CHAPTER FIVE
THE DECISION

George lay in his bed that night and listened to the sounds of the city. The celebrations had continued long into the evening, and George could still hear the bands and the crowds in the distance. He probably would have stayed out all night if his father had let him. Ever since their fight the other evening he had felt guilty about how things had turned out between the two of them. It seemed the more time he spent with the gang, the further he drifted from his father. First, the rock fight had gotten him in trouble, then he had snuck out of the house, and worst of all was the argument he had with his father when he called him a coward. He hadn't meant to hurt his father and, of course, he didn't really believe that his dad was afraid of anything. But somehow, the excitement of the prospect of war caught up with George and he said things he hadn't really meant.

It seemed they had reached a turning point in their relationship. If George signed up for the war, he might never see his father again, and even if he did, it certainly wouldn't be the same. On the other hand, if he stayed, he would lose his friends and be alone again. *What should he do?*

There was a knock on the door outside. George listened from his bed in the other room as his father got up to answer it.

"Excuse me, sir," the figure said in the doorway. "I know it's late, but my pa sent me to talk to you. He says it's extremely important and that he knows you'll listen because you've always been kind to him."

"Certainly, John," George's father said opening the door wide and waving his arm to show John a chair. "Your father told me to expect you. Come on in."

"Thank you, sir," John replied as he walked into the room. He was a tall, skinny black boy, almost as tall as George's father even though he was only 12 years old. In fact, his height allowed him to hang around with much older boys. John had spent time with George when George had no friends. The two of them had walked through the streets together, gone to the markets, and one time, John had taken George to his house near Marshall Street. George had even taught John how to throw a baseball. The two had become as close as a white and black boy in the South could get, at least until George joined the gang.

John was the son of Charles Webb, a prosperous free black living on the outskirts of Richmond. The two families knew each other through Sean's job at the Tredegar Iron Works.

As a manager, George's father was in charge of many things at the factory, one of which was to make sure that there was enough slave labor to operate the iron works. At times when labor was short, George's father had begun to hire Charles' slaves to make up the difference. He found it strange that a black man owned slaves, but once Charles explained it to him, it made sense.

"They're only slaves to you," Charles had said. "But to me they're all family, whether by blood relation or not. You see, if I keep them registered as slaves then you leave them alone. It is only when we blacks are 'free' that you all get nervous. You make us carry papers everywhere we go, limit how long we can be out at night, keep us from being outside in groups, and even prevent us from 'making noise' as you call it. You pass strange laws to prevent us from doing things like selling liquor, stop us from voting, or even testifying in court. If my 'slaves' were given their 'freedom,' they would not only have to worry about all these conditions, but they would also have to worry about a slave catcher grabbing them and selling them down South. As long as they are 'slaves' no one will kidnap my 'property' and they are safe with me. I let them keep most of the money that you pay me to rent them to your factory except for a small amount that I use to help buy other slaves. Then they can use their money for whatever they like."

George's father saw no problem with the system Charles had set up, so he had continued to hire Charles' slaves. It was the least he could do to try to compensate for this system of slavery that made him so uncomfortable. He was not an abolitionist like his deceased brother John and his wife, Regina, had been, but he still did not like the whole concept of slavery. He knew that blacks were different from whites, yet he still believed that black folks had certain rights. So whenever he could, he tried to help the slaves under his care at the factory and those he hired from men like Charles.

"So John," George heard his father begin in a friendly tone, "can I assume your father has sent you here?"

"Yes, sir," John replied nervously. "My pa says that you can help me get work."

"Well, maybe I can, John," George's father answered. "But it's not easy work you know. Of course it's better than the tobacco factory, but it's still quite difficult. You'll be working from sunrise to sunset and maybe

longer. You'll be lifting heavy barrels and metals, some
of them will be so hot they'll almost burn your hands.
You'll sweat like you've never sweated before. So much
of it will be pouring down your face that your eyes will
burn and sting, but you will not be able to wipe your
face because your hands will be busy lifting the heavy
loads. In fact, I once knew a boy your age who..."

"Sean?" a voice interrupted. "What's going on out
here? I thought you were coming to bed."

"Oh sorry, love," George's father said to his wife,
Sallie, as she walked into the room rubbing her eyes. "I
was just talking to our visitor here. It seems that—"

"What's that Negro doing here at this hour?" Sallie
shouted angrily.

"Calm down, dear, calm down," George's father
said softly as he waved both his hands up and down in
a shushing motion. "It's only Charles' son John, come
looking for a job."

"Well, couldn't he come at a more respectable
hour?" she asked. "It's past curfew by now."

"I would have, Mrs. Adams," John answered softly,
his voice filled with respect and courtesy. The last thing
he needed was Mrs. Adams losing her temper, calling
the police, and having him arrested for breaking curfew. "But all the celebrations made it difficult to get
around town. I had to take some turns into neighborhoods I didn't know and some that weren't too friendly.
I almost had to turn around but I had come so far that—"

"O.K., O.K.," George's stepmother said with a wave
of her hand. "I understand. You can stay, but make it
quick. I don't want the twins to be awakened."

John let out a sigh of relief and quietly turned back
towards George's father.

"Well, as I was saying," George's father began again.

"Is the stove still warm enough to have coffee?"
Sallie again interrupted.

"Yes, dear. But won't that keep you up?"

"I'm already up," she said gruffly. "So I might as well join you."

"We're only talking about work," George's father said matter-of-factly in an attempt to get his wife to leave the room. He hated talking about the iron works in front of her. She always had to give her opinion even though she knew nothing about the factory. Of course she was an intelligent woman. She couldn't have run her store for so long after her first husband died without being halfway knowledgeable. Sallie was always reminding him that the only reason she sold the store was to buy their house and that she did not want to embarrass him by making more money than he did.

"So what will John be doing in the factory?" Sallie began as she took a chair next to her husband.

"I'm not sure yet," George's father answered with a look of defeat on his face. It seemed as if he would have to involve his wife in the discussion after all. "I need help in several areas."

As George listened to his father describe the horrible factory work from the other room, he grew increasingly more upset. With every mention of another boring, difficult task that would only get worse as the war continued, George thought of how much he hated the factory. Day after day his father came home after dark with more stupid stories about a broken machine or a run-down worker. Even worse was the fact that his father had made him work there as well. George lost a lot of his free time because he had to work after school since the family needed the money.

In the beginning, George hadn't questioned his father about the work. Many of his friends were already working, and his cousins back in Boston always worked and had never gone to school at all. For the most part, George considered himself lucky since he only had to work part-time. But now with the possibility of war, he was beginning to think about other options.

"With the war on," George heard his father say from the other room, "we'll be needing lots more work done, John. I'm not sure how many hours we'll need you to work."

"That's right," Sallie agreed, turning towards her husband. "You'll have to convert many of the machines to make guns and artillery, won't you?"

"We may," George's father answered. "It depends on how long the war lasts."

The war! George thought to himself. *The war could be my way out!*

His mind drifted back to the conversation with the gang. It was obvious that Bobby and Bruce were planning to join the army, and the more that George listened to his father speaking with John, the more exciting the life of a soldier seemed. His head was filled with glorious visions of marching in uniform as crowds of people cheered. He thought of valiantly defending his new home of Virginia in action-packed battles and accepting the handshakes and friendship of his comrades. George felt as if he was about to burst from the excitement, and he ran into the room, interrupting his father and nearly knocking over John.

"Stop, Pa, stop!" he yelled. "I can't take it anymore. I can't listen to anymore talk of the factory. I'm going. Do you hear? I'm going to sign up to fight for Virginia!"

"W-What...why?" his father managed to say.

"Because I love Virginia," George said, his voice rising as he became more excited. "And I'm not gonna let them Northerners push us around!"

"My Lord, that's wonderful!" Sallie cried out, waving her hands towards the sky.

"What?" George's father shouted, turning towards Sallie in anger. "You approve of this?"

"Of course!" Sallie answered joyfully. "Finally we'll have someone in the family who will be defending our home."

"What's that supposed to mean?" George's father shot back in anger and defense.

"Nothing towards you, you silly man," Sallie said almost laughing. "I know that you need to stay in Richmond and work in the iron works. But now we'll have someone in our family actually at the front defending our glorious state!"

"You've got to be kidding! He's only 12 years old."

"That's old enough to be a drummer boy."

"A drummer boy," George repeated. "I ain't gonna be a drummer boy."

"A drummer is an extremely important position, George," Sallie answered quickly before George could lose his excitement. "You are right in the thick of the battle, giving out instructions with your drum to all of the soldiers. Without you, they would have no idea what to do or how to march. In a way, it's like being in command."

"Wow!" George answered.

"Then, if you're lucky, you can get promoted to combat duty."

"Stop filling his head with this nonsense!" George's father cried. "George is not going off to war!"

"I am too, Pa!" George shot back. "And you can't stop me."

"Don't you take that tone with me, young man!" his father said, raising his hand as if to strike George.

"Sean, don't!" Sallie cried. "He's only doing what he thinks is right! How can you be angry at him?"

George's father stopped his hand in mid-air and looked at George. This was his son, he thought, the only person left in the world who he truly loved more than himself. How could he hit him? George was all he had remaining of his first wife, Elizabeth. George was his pride and joy. He was a good boy, a brave boy, and Sallie was right. He was only doing what he thought was right.

"Son, if this is because of our fight the other day or because of the work at the factory, we can do something about that."

"No, Pa," George responded softly with love and respect. He also felt sad that they almost had another fight and he was determined to avoid one this time. "Well, not really anyhow. I have been thinking about this for a while now. A lot of my friends have already decided to sign up, and I can't sit back and let our home be invaded by them Yankees. We can't let them tell us how to live and how to run our lives. We got to defend our rights!"

"What rights are those, sir?" John interrupted quietly. He had been sitting in the same chair listening patiently to George and his father. He had not wanted to say anything, and at one point he almost left. But he found he could not keep quiet while they argued over something as important to him as this.

"The right to make up our own minds, of course," George replied softly. He had been surprised by John's interruption and found it hard to answer quickly. "The right to rule ourselves and to not be ruled by a president we did not elect."

"And the right to own slaves?" John asked.

"Well, of course," George replied awkwardly. "But listen hear, John. This war is not over slavery, so you don't need to be concerned. It's over our right to make our own decisions. It's over the Constitution and tyranny. We're fighting to be free from Mr. Lincoln just as George Washington fought to be free from horrid King George. Why, some people have called this the second American Revolution!"

"With all due respect," John continued, "it seems to me that you would not be arguing so much with them Northerners if you didn't have slavery separating you in the first place."

"You may be right, John," George's father interrupted. "I've lived in both the North and the South, and I've seen how slavery has made life in the South much different than life in the North. Certainly that is a large part of what makes us argue. However, the boys who go off to fight and those of us who stay behind to work are not defending our land just to keep you in slavery."

"That's right," George added. "I am not going to die just so a rich guy can keep you in slavery; I am fighting over the right to decide for ourselves."

"Well, sirs," John said. "Respectfully, I must say that this big difference you have is no difference to me. You are going to fight them Northerners. If you win, I will remain a slave. If you lose, then maybe them Northerners will see to it that I am freed."

"Well, say what you like," George said in an annoyed voice. "But we ain't gonna lose."

CHAPTER SIX
SOLDIERS

"George! George!" Eric yelled as he stormed into the tent. His red hair was flying all over his face, and he held a large brown package tightly with both arms. "Look what just came for you!"

George turned around quickly and tried to stand but his aching muscles responded slowly. He had just finished another boring day of drills and chores and had only just lain down to rest five minutes ago.

"What is it?" George asked. His voice was filled with excitement and surprise. He had never received a package before, only letters. It seemed that every soldier in the army received letters from someone. Whether it was news from home or everyday conversation about the weather, these letters made the soldiers feel like people again. Usually the letters were from family members, but sometimes they were from women or girls the soldiers did not know at all. It seemed that the women back home had taken it upon themselves to write letters to as many soldiers as they could. They wanted to try to make the men and boys realize how much they were appreciated and loved. George and his dad wrote to each other regularly, and George had even received several letters from two girls in Richmond.

"I don't know," Eric answered, setting the package down on the ground. "But it looks like it comes from Richmond. Think it's from your dad?"

"I doubt it," George responded as he slowly stood up and looked down at Eric. George had grown quickly during the past year in the army. His muscles had filled out and his legs had sprouted like weeds. He was now taller and heavier than Eric and most of his friends. He still looked like an unfinished painting, as different parts of his body had not grown at the same rate. His chest was still small and hairless even though he had already begun to shave his face. His feet had not grown much at all, which caused him to stumble because of his new body weight.

"Maybe it's from one of those girls again!" Eric said with enthusiasm. The boys had been excited when they started getting letters from strange girls in Richmond, and they had already begun dreaming about meeting up with them. One boy had even run off to find his girl, but he was caught and punished before he made it out of camp.

"Maybe," George repeated, looking at the box one last time.

"Open it!" Eric begged.

George slowly pulled at the strings that held the box closed as he wondered what was inside. Was it a new uniform? The one he had never fit him properly although it had been made for him personally by his stepmother. Maybe it was some food! All he ever seemed to get in the army was cornbread, hardtack, or potatoes. Perhaps it was even a book. He couldn't remember the last time he had read to the others. With all the boring time between battles, they needed something to do and they couldn't play cards all of the time.

"Socks!" George yelled with joy as he pulled a clean fresh pair of homespun white socks from the box. "I got me a new pair of socks!"

"Wow!" Eric said jealously. "You lucky dog."

"I can't remember what it feels like to have a warm pair of socks on my feet," George said happily. "I've got so many holes in these ones that I'm not sure how to put them on."

"I know what you mean," Eric added. "Every time I walk I feel the inside of my shoe rubbing against my toes. I've lost most of the skin on my piggy toe and the rest of them are permanently bruised."

"Well, you can have my old ones for what they're worth," George offered. "Maybe you can sew the two together to make one decent pair."

"Gee thanks," Eric replied sincerely. "But what else is in there? That box is too big for just a pair of socks."

"Hmmmm," George said as he reached into the box.

"Hey, here's a letter!" he said after a second or two.

"What does it say?" Eric asked.

George looked at him.

"That is," Eric said awkwardly, "if you don't mind reading it to me."

George smiled.

"Nahhh, I don't mind." George had gotten used to reading letters for the other boys and men of his company who couldn't read. He had even written several letters for Eric and a few others.

"Wow," George said softly as he looked down at the paper. "It's from Sallie!"

"Sallie?" Eric asked.

"My stepmom," George replied. "I ain't never got a letter from her, never mind a package."

"Well, what does it say?...what does it say?" Eric begged.

George sat down, unfolded the letter, and began to read out loud.

October 1862.

Dearest George:

Please forgive me for not writing you in the past. I have wanted to for so long but did not want to intrude on the special relationship you have with your father. He is such a special man and he loves you so much, but I could not help but write after I heard the wonderful news of your promotion from drummer boy to regular infantry soldier.

We are all soooo proud of you here! Ever since you left, my friends and I have been discussing how brave you boys were to go off and fight the horrid Yankee invaders. You looked so dashing and mature in your uniform when you marched past us that last day before you went off to fight.

Please understand that we all are doing everything that we can to support you brave boys fighting for our homes. We thought that all was lost when the Federals marched on the city, but somehow you and General Lee managed to push them back and save our fair city! Then, when you took the war to them by going into Maryland and attacking the Federals at Sharpsburg[1] we cried for all our poor dead. And still you boys continue fighting!

I'm not sure how you do it. We have seen so many dead and wounded brought to Richmond and set up in makeshift hospitals that the city has become more of a living nightmare than the beautiful, thriving capital it was only two years ago.

Remember the Calhoun house down the street? It was turned into a boardinghouse for all of the refugees running from the Yankees. There is trash all over the street, and strangers in every place we walk. Many of these people are, of course, destitute and homeless. Their homes and livelihoods have been

---

1. The Southerners called this the battle of Sharpsburg. The Northerners referred to it as the battle of Antietam.

*destroyed if not by the soldiers themselves then by
the terrible blockade of ships that have prevented
almost all trade.*

*I have to pay twice as much for coffee, if I can get
it at all. Cotton and wool have doubled in price so
much that I was only able to make you one pair of
socks instead of two. The twins have had to get used
to honey on their food instead of sugar since there is
none to be found in the whole city!*

*But I don't mean to complain. No matter how
much we suffer, I'm sure it is nothing compared to
what you must be going through. We have heard of
the terrible battles, seen the many caskets built for
your comrades, and heard the stories of your lack of
supplies.*

*We are doing all that we can to help you, you
must understand that. The ladies of Richmond are
raising money, sewing uniforms, or baking food to
send to our boys.*

The apples in the box—

"Apples?" Eric interrupted. "There are apples in
there?"

"I don't know," George answered. "Let's look."

George put the letter down, stood up, and reached
into the box again.

"Wow!" he cried, pulling out a bag of apples.
"There's a whole bag of them!"

"You lucky dog!"

"And there's other stuff too!" George said gleefully
as he pulled more containers out of the box. "There's
apple butter and I think some cookies!"

"Apple butter?" Eric said. "Wow, you can spread
that on the stale bread they give out and finally make
it taste half-decent."

"Yeah!"

"Is there anything else?" Eric asked as he peered
over George's shoulder and tried to look into the box.

"No, that's it," George answered.

"Well," Eric began slowly, "whatcha gonna do with all that food?"

"Gee, I dunno," George said thoughtfully. He realized what a difficult position he was in now. "I suppose I should share it but there ain't enough to go around for the whole company. I certainly can't hide it. Even if I wanted to, which I don't, someone is bound to find out."

"Why don't you draw lots to see who gets it," Eric suggested. "And of course keep a little more for yourself, just like everyone does."

"And for you," George grinned as he handed Eric an apple.

"Gee thanks, George!" Eric said sincerely.

"No problem," George answered as he took a bite of the beautiful, red, Ablemarle apple. "Anything for a buddy."

"Mmm," Eric mumbled through a big bite. The juice sprayed into the air and the crunch was so loud that Eric shrunk back a little, afraid that someone had heard it. "Thish is the besh apple I think I've ebber had."

"Yeah," George agreed through giggles, "me too."

The two of them sat down and ate. They didn't speak or move, they just ate. With each bite, more delicious juice flowed out of the apple, into their mouths, and sometimes down their cheeks. The crunching of the apple skin as their teeth sunk in only heightened the pleasure of each bite. When they reached the core, they slowly ate every little piece, making sure not to lose any on the ground. Eric even took little bites as if he were a chipmunk so as not to miss any possible piece of apple.

George laughed at him and boastfully called, "Watch this!" as he threw the remaining apple, core and all, into his mouth.

"Disgusting!" Eric shouted.

"Want a cookie?" George said playfully.

"What kind?" Eric asked.

"I don't know."

"Pick up the letter and see," Eric reminded him. "You never finished it anyway."

"Where was I?" George asked out loud as he scanned the letter to see where he left off. "Oh yeah."

> The apples in the box were picked locally, of course, and they are your favorite variety, at least your father says so.
>
> Speaking of your father, he sends his love and wants you to know how proud he is of you as well. I know that the two of you did not part on the happiest of terms, but as you must know by now after all the letters that you two have exchanged, he has always been extremely proud of you and he understands and respects what you decided to do. Perhaps he was against your joining up in the beginning not because he was against the war, but because he was afraid of losing you.
>
> I can tell you now that as far as your father's patriotism goes he is as dedicated to our cause as any Southern man could be. Not only has he been working day and night at the iron works to supply you boys with weapons, but he has also joined a local militia at the iron works. When he is not working, he is drilling and practicing in case the dreaded Yankees return to attack our fair city. I must say, George, that I am so impressed with him and you. You two may have moved to Richmond from the North several years ago, but you have both proven to be Southerners at heart.

"From the North?" Eric interrupted again. "I thought you said you were from Kansas?"

"Uh...well, I was," George answered awkwardly. Despite the fact that he had been with Eric and the others for almost two years now, he had never gotten around to telling them the whole story. "But before that my dad and I lived in Boston."

"Boston?" Eric repeated. "Where all them abolitionists live?"

"Yeah," George said quickly before Eric could panic, "but we left because of all them abolitionists. After the whole John Brown thing we decided we didn't want to return to Boston and we moved to Richmond."

"Well, how come you never told us?" Eric asked.

"I dunno," George answered. "I guess it just never came up. You're not angry, are you?"

Eric was silent for a moment as he considered.

"Nahhh," he said finally. "We been through too much for me too be angry at you. If I was in your shoes I probably would have done the same thing."

The boys sat quietly for a minute, unsure of what to say or do next.

"So you gonna tell everyone?" Eric asked.

"About being from Boston?" George asked.

"Naahhhh," Eric said with a wave of his hand. "That ain't no big deal. They'll find out eventually. Are you gonna tell 'em about the apples and the cookies?"

"Oh that," George grinned. "Well yeah, of course. In fact, why don't you go round up some of 'em now while I finish reading my letter."

"O.K.," Eric agreed as he stood and walked out of the tent. "I'll be back in a few minutes. Don't eat any more while I'm gone."

"I won't!" George called back with a smile. Then he turned his attention back to the letter he was still holding and continued to read.

As far as your question about General Pickett goes, your father and I have asked around but not many people know about him. With all the army reorganizations General Lee has ordered recently, it has become quite confusing for us here at home. We have had to rewrite many of our letters and resend several uniforms, but from what I can gather, General Pickett should make a fine commander of your division. After all, if both Generals Longstreet and Lee believe in him then he must be a competent commander.

Well, George, it is about time for me to leave. I hope this letter has lightened your spirits somewhat. Use the socks and food well and please try your best to continue. You are all your father has and you are all Virginia has.

Stay well,

Love,

Sallie

CHAPTER SEVEN
THE PRANK

"Mmmm," Bruce grinned as he took another bite. "These cookies are delicious, George. Your stepmom sure can cook."

"Yeah George," Russell agreed. "These are the best cookies I've ever had."

"Thanks, guys," George replied, looking around at the 20 or so ragged-looking, overworked soldiers. It was the end of yet another cold November day in Virginia, and everyone was sitting or standing around the campfire trying to stay warm. After a long day of chores and drills, it was difficult for aching muscles to stay warm. The boys' uniforms did little to keep out the cold. Their homespun cotton shirts, woolen socks, and jackets were the only things the soldiers had to wear all of the time. After more than a year of marching, working, and fighting, the clothes were drenched in sweat and dirt and riddled with many holes.

George rubbed his hands together as he held them in front of the fire. It was at times like this that George felt the closest to his friends in the regiment. He had made many new friends since he joined last year, but what was more amazing was that so many of his buddies from the old gang were in his company. It was very common for men and boys from the same town to be put together in one unit, but George found it incredible that Bruce, Bobby, Russell, Steven, John, his Richmond neighbor Mike and, of course, George's best friend Eric were all still with him.

George had also made new friends. Scattered throughout the company were boys from other areas of Richmond and from other gangs. The younger boys tended to separate themselves from the older ones, but there were still plenty of 18-, 19-, and 20-year-old boys who hung out with George.

They had been through so much together, George thought, as he looked around at his new and old friends. *They had marched hundreds of miles in the snow, rain, and mud, across rivers and mountains, and through forests and farmland. They had drilled repeatedly day after day. They had gone out in search parties foraging for food when the army couldn't feed them. They had fought back the Yankee invaders numerous times, pushing them out of Virginia and claiming many victories. All of these things had created a strong bond among these boys and young men that George had previously thought was only possible between him and his father.*

These guys are my family, George realized with a smile. His thoughts drifted in and out of the conversations around the fire as he sat back quietly and wondered about what was going on around him. He looked to his right and saw Jason and Russell fighting over the last cookie.

They're always fighting over something, George thought, with a roll of his eyes. *If it isn't over where the army is heading or what chore will be assigned next, then it's over which girl back in Richmond is prettier, or what Yankee army is the stupidest. No matter what, it seems that they are always calling each other names and making the rest of us laugh.*

Look at Mike over there, George thought, as he turned his eyes to his left. *He's just laughing away like the rest of 'em. You'd never know that his cousin died just the other day. But then again, that's what is so funny about all of this. You don't waste time thinking much about whom you lost 'cause you lost so many. Lord, back at Sharpsburg we lost thousands and thousands of men, and them Yankees probably lost even more. I don't know, what keeps those Blue bellies going after they keep losing. If they don't stop coming after us real soon there ain't gonna be anyone left on either side.*

"Hey, guys, look who I found!" Bobby shouted, interrupting George's thoughts as he approached the campfire with another soldier.

"Peter!" Bruce yelled, turning his head and standing to greet the new recruit. "What are you doing here? We all thought you weren't gonna sign up!"

"I didn't," Peter said simply.

"Huh?" Bruce wondered. "Then how come—"

"He got drafted!" Russell yelled from his position on the other side of the fire.

"Drafted?" Jason repeated as he grabbed the cookie from Russell one last time.

"Yeah," Russell answered, flailing his arms around and trying to grab the cookie that Jason was waving teasingly back and forth. "Remember the Congress passed it some months back cuz we needed more men?"

"Oh yeah," Jason recalled as he stuffed the cookie in his mouth and continued mumbling through the bites and spitting cookie crumbs as he talked. "But how come you know dish guy? We've had plenty of recruits here before and you never paid no attenshun to dem."

"That's cuz Peter here was in our gang back home," Bobby answered for Russell.

"Which gang?" Jason asked. Although he was also from Richmond he had never been a member of any of the gangs. "Oh, you mean the Gamble Hill Cats gang that you guys said you were in before the war?"

"That's right," Bobby answered. "And Peter here was in the gang with us. At least until we all signed up to fight and Peter chickened out."

"I didn't chicken out," Peter quickly replied before the others could get angry. "My dad was against the war and he said I couldn't go."

"You could've just run away like I did," Steven sneered.

"No, I couldn't," Peter answered. "I don't look as old as you and the recruiting officer wouldn't believe I was old enough without my dad there."

"You should have grabbed some stranger and asked him to lie for you like I did," Jason said, wiping his mouth clean of the last cookie. "Then your old man couldn't have stopped you."

"I didn't think of that," Peter said softly.

"I think he didn't join because he's against this war just like his old man is!" Bruce said with his finger pointed directly at Peter. "He always talked about how he was against secession and he didn't want us to throw eggs at the convention when they were talking about it. Remember?"

"Yeah!" George and Stephen agreed.

"Wait a minute, you guys," Russell interrupted, trying to calm things down. "I didn't want to throw those eggs either. In fact, a lot of us here were against secession in the beginning. Just because Peter was, doesn't make him a Yankee."

"Yeah maybe," George agreed, remembering his father's opposition to secession as well.

"Well, I'm not sure I can trust him," Bruce went on. "How are we gonna leave our backs to a soldier who may or may not be a Yank?"

"I ain't no Yankee!" Peter yelled loud enough for everyone to hear. He really was angry at the accusation, but he was also afraid that if he did not set the record straight, he would always be an outsider among them. "I'm as loyal as any of you. I really wanted to join up with you, I really did! And when my dad said I couldn't, I didn't know what else to do. So I helped out in the city, putting packages together for you guys, volunteering in the hospitals, and doing anything else I could to help out."

The boys all looked at Peter quietly. Maybe he was telling the truth. They couldn't imagine what it must be like to be stuck at home while everyone else is off defending the country. Peter must have felt really alone.

"Besides," Peter continued while he still had their attention, "if I really didn't want to fight, I could have hired a substitute in my place. Y'all know that my dad has enough money to pay my way out."

"That's true," Russell added. "The government said that you could send money instead of your sons. Remember?"

"Rich man's war, poor man's fight," George, Eric, and Stephen all said simultaneously. The phrase had caught on quickly among the mostly poor, nonslave-holding soldiers. Some found it strange that these boys and men were fighting for the right to own slaves when they held none of their own. But as George had said to John several years ago, they were fighting for the right to decide on their own what they wanted to do about slavery.

"So," Bobby interjected, "I guess we should all welcome Peter to the regiment. Let's do something fun, huh guys?"

"Let's play baseball!" someone shouted.

"Let's go find some girls!" yelled another.

"Girls?" Bruce said smartly. "Where you gonna find girls on a cold winter day like this one?"

"I got an idea," a taller soldier said as he pushed his way to the front of the circle. "Let's go smoke out a religious meeting."

"Kevin?" Peter shouted out loud in surprise, as he recognized the tall soldier. "Kevin Pender, the leader of the Fifth Street Cats?"

"Yeah, it's me," Kevin said simply. "Surprised?"

"Well, yeah," Peter said slowly. "I knew you joined up, but I never expected you to be here and I certainly never thought—"

"That I'd be getting along with you Gambles Hill Cats?" Kevin finished for Peter.

"Uh...yeah," Peter replied.

"All that stuff's forgotten, Peter," Russell said quickly. "We're soldiers now. There ain't no room for silly gang fights here."

"Well no, of course not," Peter said awkwardly.

"You'll catch on soon enough, Peter," Eric said. "You'll see that we're all in this together. In a way we're only one bigger gang now, fighting for a much bigger territory, only this time it's to the death."

"Yeah, well, on that note," Bobby said breaking the sudden, awkward silence following Eric's comment. "Let's go back to having some fun. Kevin, what's your idea?"

"Well," Kevin began, "you know how the sergeant and his friends are really getting into this religion thing?"

"Yeah," the boys said slowly. They were a little hesitant to talk about religion. It was a very personal thing to all of them and many days it seemed as if their religion was the only thing keeping them alive. In fact, soldiers throughout the army were becoming more and more observant as the war continued.

"And you know all the jokes they've pulled on us lately, right?"

"Right!" the boys added a little more enthusiastically this time. They had become pretty annoyed at all the tricks the sergeant and his buddies had played on them recently. With all the free time they had, the soldiers found plenty of ways to pull pranks on each other, such as putting bugs in shoes and beds, soot on razor blades, and grease on their combs. It was getting so that you had to watch everything you did.

"O.K., here's what we do," Kevin said as he kneeled down and drew his plan in the dirt. "We use one of our big tents and build a dirt chimney like the ones some of those Alabama boys have. Then, we get the minister and invite the sergeant and his buddies to a special service."

"What's so great about that?" George asked.

"I'm not done yet," Kevin said shaking his head. "Then, we get four or five of us to sing in the choir. While they are singing, I'll take Russell or George here... who's smaller?"

"I am!" Russell said raising his hand real fast.

"But you're fat!" George quickly yelled out.

The boys all laughed.

Russell looked away.

"O.K., George then," Kevin continued touching George lightly on the chest. "He'll get behind the chimney with a bucket of water and I'll lift him near the mouth of it. Then when the choir sings 'Scotland's burning, Cast on water,' George will drop the water on the fire and that will shoot smoke and embers everywhere!"

"They'll be covered with it!" Bruce yelled in excitement.

"Yeah!" Bobby agreed. "What a great idea! They'll be so busy cleaning their uniforms that they'll leave us alone for at least a day or two."

"So?" Kevin asked. "You guys in?"

"Yeah!" they all shouted.

It didn't take long to build the chimney and get the plan in motion. The only problem, Russell pointed out, was that the boys would get covered in smoke too. But Kevin figured if they get behind the larger men in the front and scattered out of the tent just before the fire was put out, they wouldn't get blackened as the others would.

By the time the minister finally arrived, everything was set. Russell, Eric, Jason, Peter, and Stephen stood as the choir; Kevin and George hid in the back near the water bucket; and the rest of the boys stood towards the entrance away from the chimney. Things went along smoothly and the service was actually quite beautiful. At one point George even wondered whether they should really be doing what they were planning. But as the service neared the end, George thought again of the smoke and embers covering everyone and he smiled and waited for his chance.

George grabbed the bucket of water. Kevin lifted him up. The choir began to sing. George listened intently, waiting for the key words.

"Scotland's burning! Cast on water!"

Instantly, George poured the water down the chimney where it landed right in the middle of the fire. The boys all screamed and ran out of the tent while the men looked around in confusion. Within seconds, a huge cloud of smoke immediately shot into the tent carrying embers and ash everywhere.

"Aaggghhh!" the boys heard the men screaming. Shouts and curses billowed out of the tent.

"What the—"

"Hey!"

"I can't see!"

"Get out, get out!"

The boys all laughed and pointed as their victims came charging out of the tent, coughing, wheezing, and waving their hands violently in front of them trying to clear away the smoke. As the air began to clear, the boys laughed even harder when they saw that the men's faces were completely blackened, their hair filled with wood and ash, and their uniforms stained and dirty.

"Whose idea was this?" the sergeant growled between coughs. "I demand to know who put you all up to this."

The boys just continued to laugh and point at the blackened, charcoal-covered soldiers.

"I'm warning you!" the sergeant threatened.

"What's going on here?" a loud voice suddenly interrupted. All heads turned in the direction of the sound to see General Kemper standing in the midst of all the chaos. His arms were folded across his chest, and he was wearing a frown that showed he was not in the least pleased with what he was watching.

"G-g-g-general, sir," the sergeant began with an awkward salute. "What are you doing here? We thought you were in a meeting, sir."

"I *was* in a meeting," the general began slowly, looking around at the men in a curious stare. It was not totally uncommon for officers to wander into the enlisted men's camp or even to talk with them for a while, but this was the first time that George had been so close to General Kemper in a casual manner. He was a tough-looking man with a long, shaggy black beard that grew down to his chest and completely hid his mouth from view. His hair was combed back to reveal a large forehead, and his eyes were set back deeply behind his slightly wider than average nose.

"Yes, sir," the sergeant said quickly, saluting again and standing at attention. He was a ridiculous sight, standing stiff as a board, his face covered in soot, his hair standing on end, and his uniform black and ruffled. The general had to concentrate hard to keep from laughing.

"You boys having some fun?" he asked with a slight hint of a smile.

"Y-yes, sir," the sergeant answered. "Well, that is some of us are."

"I would assume by the condition of your uniform," the general continued, "that you are not one of the men having fun."

"N-no, sir," the sergeant answered simply. He had no desire to get into the details of this little embarrassment.

"It's just as well that you get this behavior out of your system now," the general said with a shrug of his shoulders. He really was not upset about the prank; in fact, the officers had often laughed at the many jokes the men pulled on each other. It kept them happy; and a happy soldier was a good soldier.

"Sir?" the sergeant asked in confusion. He was not exactly sure what the general meant.

"You'll hear the details soon enough," the general answered as he began to walk away. "But I can tell you that we've heard the Federals are on the move and we've been ordered to pursue them."

The soldiers all looked at each other in silence. The jokes were forgotten, the dirty uniforms were forgotten, and the anger was forgotten. None of it mattered anymore. They were moving out.

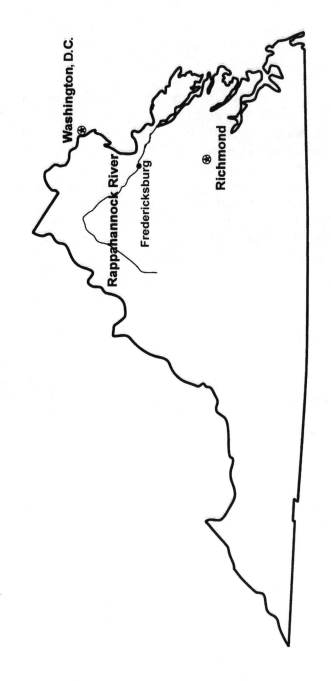

CHAPTER EIGHT
BOMBS

Kaboom, kaboom, kaboom!

Allison jumped back from the kitchen table and dropped the potato she had been peeling for breakfast as the windows shook from the sudden explosions.

"What was that, Mommy?" she cried out nervously.

"I don't know, dear," Allison's mother answered slowly, staring up from her work of cutting the vegetables and looking out the window. "But you'd better go wake your father."

Allison stopped doing her chores and headed to her father's room. It had been over two weeks since the Federal army had arrived outside the city of Fredericksburg, and she had been hoping that they would eventually move on as they had before. She, her father, and her mother had already left the city once when an evacuation was declared, and she was not looking forward to doing it again—especially in the middle of the winter.

"Daddy, daddy," Allison called as she shook her father's shoulders. "There's been some cannon noises. Wake up, wake up!"

"Huh?" her father responded sleepily as he rubbed his eyes and lifted his head. "When? Where?"

"I don't know," Allison answered. "It sounded as if it was coming from General Lee's troops up on the hills."

"General Lee?" her father repeated.

"I think so," Allison answered. "It didn't sound like it was from across the river where the Federals are."

"Well, don't worry about it, dear," her father said quickly as he stood up and began to dress. "I'm sure he's just testing his guns."

"Are we gonna have to leave?" she asked softly. Her young voice was shaky as her big blue eyes stared up at her father.

"No, no," her father answered as he gently rubbed the long blond hair on top of Allison's head.

"But everyone else has," she answered quickly.

"Not everyone," her father replied. "There are the Beales and the Johnsons and many other families who have decided to stay."

He approached his daughter and picked her up in his arms. Although she was already 9 years old, he could still lift her up and hold her up to his face. "Now don't you worry," he said, staring into her eyes, "everything's going to be O.K."

Allison didn't say a word, but her father could tell that she was still scared. He tried to act calm and unconcerned as he put her back down and kissed her on the top of her head. "Now, you go back to the kitchen and tell mommy that I'll be right out."

"O.K.," Allison answered as her father gently tapped her lightly on the bottom to move her towards the door.

"Mommy," Allison said as she returned to the kitchen. "Daddy says not to worry and that he'll be right out."

"Thank you, dear," Allison's mother answered from the window. She had stopped preparing breakfast completely and was staring intently out at the city trying to discover what was happening.

Kaboom! Both of them jumped back as another explosion shattered the quiet morning air.

"Can you see anything?" Allison asked anxiously while her mother stuck her nose to the window and turned her head back and forth looking for the source of the noise.

"No, not yet," she answered.

"I'm going to go outside and look," Allison said, turning away from her mother and running out the front door.

"Allison, no!" her mother cried, turning around and waving her hands in vain.

Ignoring her mother, Allison opened the door and ran into the front yard. The morning air was crisp and cold especially in her bare feet. She took a deep breath and watched as the mist from her mouth billowed out into the coolness. She looked around. Nothing seemed to be happening. The usual noises of people coming and going, birds singing in the air, and dogs barking were gone. An eerie silence hung over the city.

"Allison, get back in here," her mother called angrily from the doorstep.

"But mother," Allison answered. "There's nothing going on."

"It's still not a good idea to be out here," her mother answered as she joined Allison in the yard.

The two of them stared silently into the air looking for some sign of what was happening.

"What's that?" Allison asked curiously as she pointed to a sudden flash of light coming from across the river.

"What?" her mother asked. "I don't see—"

An intense whistling sound pierced the silence and forced Allison to cover her ears.

"Get down!" her mother screamed, pushing Allison down to the ground.

Allison's face hit the dirt. An explosion vibrated through her body. Dirt and wood flew everywhere. Her mother screamed. Allison turned her head and saw her mother fall next to her.

"Mother!" she screamed.

Kaboom, kaboom, kaboom! The air vibrated with the terrible thunder of more cannon fire. Allison smothered her face into the dirt and covered her head with both her hands. The high-pitched whistling came again. Allison thought her ears would burst. Explosions fired all around her as more dirt, wood, and glass went flying through the air.

"Allison!" she heard her father call from the house. "Jane!"

"Daddy!" Allison screamed over the explosions as she lifted her head and saw her father appear in the doorway.

He looked around for a second or two until he saw them lying in the dirt. "My Lord!" he cried as he ran towards them.

Kaboom, kaboom, kaboom! He bent his head and continued to run.

"Allison, are you alright?" her father shouted as he knelt beside her.

"I...I think so," she answered. "But I think Mommy's hurt."

"Jane?" Allison's father said, turning towards his wife.

"She pushed me down just as the cannon exploded," Allison explained. "I heard her scream and she fell right there."

"Jane?" Allison's father repeated. "Are you alright?"

Allison's mother moaned as her husband shook her slowly. More cannon shells landed nearby. Allison turned and saw the exterior of her neighbor's house collapse.

"We've got to get out of here!" Allison's father yelled as he picked up her mother and slowly stood up. "Follow me," he shouted. "And keep your head down."

They ran towards the house as fast as they could. The cannons continued to fire. With each kaboom! Allison bent her head down further and fell backwards a step or two.

"C'mon!" Allison's father shouted. He was struggling to hold up his wife amidst the smoke and the dirt and the debris flying through the air. "You've got to run faster!"

With a burst of speed and determination, Allison gritted her teeth, closed her eyes, and ran towards the house. Her father followed close behind and once inside, they made their way down into the cellar where Allison's father laid her mother on a blanket. The shelling continued to pound the ground, and the vibrations and noise were constant but at least they were not in the direct line of fire anymore.

"We'll be safe here for now," he said in between breaths. Both of them were panting hard, and Allison's heart was beating so fast she thought it would break its way right through her chest.

"But the house is still shaking, and I can still hear the terrible explosions," Allison cried.

There was a sudden crash and small pieces of wood and dust from the ceiling fell into the cellar.

"It's the best we can do for now," Allison's father answered as he coughed a little and waved the dust from in front of his face. "Just keep your head down and your ears covered and hopefully we'll be alright."

"What about Mommy?" Allison asked.

"She'll be alright, dear," he tried to reassure her as he knelt next to his wife and tried to make her comfortable. "You go ahead and light the candle so we can see just what's going on."

He patted down the blanket his wife was resting on and slowly massaged her body. Allison lit the candle and brought it to the middle of the room.

"Is she O.K.?" Allison asked holding the candle near her mother's face. She could see how pale her mother's skin was even through all of the dirt and mud that covered her cheeks.

"I'm sure she is," her father answered. "She's just...oh-h-h."

"What's that?" Allison cried in alarm when her father fell backwards.

"My Lord," he said softly as he held his bloody hand up to the light. "She's been hit."

"Hit?" Allison repeated. "Hit...oh my God!"

"Calm down, calm down," Allison's father said, wiping his hand clean and grabbing both of Allison's arms at the elbows. He held her gently but firmly and stared directly into her eyes. "You've got to be brave for Mommy, Allison. It's the only way we can save her. We're in a terrible situation and we can pull through if we keep our heads and work together. Do you understand?"

"Uh-huh," Allison nodded slowly. The house shook again and more pieces of the ceiling came crashing down. Allison coughed and then she took a deep breath. Tears began to well up in her eyes but she fought desperately to hold them back. She sniffed once or twice and took another deep breath. She would not scream. She would be brave for her mommy.

"Good girl," her father said after giving her a tight hug and standing up. "Why don't you go over to the shelf and grab me some napkins and towels that I can use to comfort your mother and dry up this blood."

The pounding from the cannonballs continued. Pieces of the ceiling kept falling on them. More than once, Allison had to protect her mother's body from falling debris. She tried to cover her ears as much as possible, but eventually her arms grew tired and she had to let them down. She wanted to yell. She wanted to run and hide but there was nowhere to go. Several times during the morning she began to cry until the tears would come no more and then she would just sob lightly. At one point a cannonball crashed into the cellar and almost hit her father as he knelt beside her mother. Some time around noon she was beginning to wonder whether it would ever end. She couldn't take the constant noise much longer.

"She's getting worse," Allison's father said softly. He was unsure if he wanted Allison to know how bad off her mother was.

"What can we do?" Allison cried.

"We've got to get her some water to start," he answered. "Then, we've got to get her some bandages and a doctor."

"But how?" Allison whined. "The cannons are still firing and the house is still shaking."

"I don't know," he answered. "But we've got to try soon."

The pounding continued. This time was even worse though, as Allison watched her mother roll back and forth and moan in her semiconscious state.

"Ohhhhhh," she moaned.

Allison went over to her.

"Ohhhhh," she moaned again.

"It's alright, Mommy," Allison said softly, stroking her mother's soft brown hair. "It will be over soon and we'll get you some help."

"Allison?" her mother said abruptly. She lifted her head up.

"Jane?" Allison's father gasped.

She turned towards her husband and smiled.

"Hi," she said in a voice not much louder than a whisper.

"How do you feel," he asked softly as he stroked her hair with his left hand.

"Tired," she answered after a second or two. "Tired and thirsty." She tried to lift up her head. "Ohhh," she moaned as her head fell back onto the blanket.

"You've got to save your strength," her husband said in a worried voice. Allison noticed his hand shaking a little as he gently put a pillow under her mother's head.

"Ron?" she asked as she looked towards her husband.

"We're both here, Mommy," Allison said comfortingly. "We're both here to take care of you."

Allison's mother smiled. She grabbed Allison's little hand in hers and tightly squeezed it. She stared into her daughter's eyes and Allison could see the strength inside of her. She knew that her mother would not give up.

"Ohhhh," she moaned again. She closed her eyes and began to roll from side to side.

Allison looked at her father in alarm. He stared at her blankly, unsure of what to say or do. The cannons continued to fire.

"Water," Allison's mother gasped, her voice barely above a whisper, "water."

"We've got to do something, Daddy," Allison cried.

"I know, I know," he said firmly. He looked around. He looked at his wife then at Allison. "I've got to go upstairs."

"But Daddy!" Allison screamed as she jumped up to her feet. "You'll be killed!"

"I've got to try," he said slowly. His voice sounded shaky, not so much from fear but from indecision. If he did go and find some water and bandages he might be able to save his wife, but if something happened to him then Allison would be all alone. What should he do? He looked at Allison. He looked at his wife, lying in the dark, damp cellar, moaning and writhing and slowly dying. Then, suddenly, he looked up at the ceiling and stared.

"Daddy?" Allison asked.

"Sssshhhh," he said softly, holding his finger to his lips.

Allison looked around as well. The cannons had stopped! It was over!

"They've stopped!" she yelled and jumped and yelled. "They've stopped!"

"Stay here with your mother," her father commanded quickly. Without a second's hesitation he bounded up the stairs and out of the cellar before Allison had even finished celebrating.

"It's over, it's over," Allison said gleefully to her mother as she bent down to comfort her. "Daddy will go get you help and everything will be alright."

Her mother didn't answer. She just continued to moan softly and roll back and forth. *But that was O.K.,* Allison thought to herself. *Daddy would be back soon.*

RUINS OF FREDERICKSBURG

CHAPTER NINE
THE LOOTING

"Allison, the town is on fire!" she heard her father call down to her from upstairs after almost an hour of waiting. He had come down once to bring Allison's mother some water, but he had returned upstairs to try to find out what was going on outside and to get more water and bandages for her mother. "Ambulances are on their way, but the Yankees are coming and we have to get out of here quick!"

"What should I do?" she called back to her father. Her mother had stopped moaning and was completely quiet now. Allison was afraid she was dead, but when she put her ear to her chest she could still hear her mother's heartbeat even though it was faint.

"Just wait another minute or two!" her father answered. "I have to get some water and some towels from the kitchen. I'll be right down."

"O.K.," Allison called back to him. She heard her father walk away from the door and go into the kitchen. Then she put her head back down on her mother's chest and waited.

After a few minutes of listening to her father frantically banging around the kitchen, she heard him yell. "I've got it all. I'll be right down!"

Allison lifted her head up again and watched the door to see her father return.

Kaboom, kaboom, kaboom, kaboom, kaboom! The cannons roared again even more rapidly than before. "Daddy!" Allison screamed.

Kaboom, kaboom, kaboom, kaboom! The whole house shook and Allison heard the crashing down of ceilings and walls.

"Daddy!" she screamed again.

The shelling continued. Allison lowered her head deep into her mother's chest to try to escape the noise but it did little good. With every explosion her whole body shook and flinched. What could she do? What was going to happen? She began to cry.

"Mommy, mommy," she wailed. "Please wake up. Please tell me what to do?"

Kaboom, kaboom, kaboom! Allison continued to cry.

Then a hand softly rubbed the back of her head.

"Allison?" her mother suddenly said. "What's wrong, dear?"

"Oh Mommy," Allison cried. She felt a mixture of relief and fear now that her mother was awake. "The cannons are all firing at us, and Daddy was upstairs and now he's gone, and I don't know what to do."

"Don't worry," her mother said softly as she continued to stroke the back of her head. "Mommy will take care of you."

Allison smiled back and tightly hugged her mother. Even though the shells never stopped falling and the noises grew even louder, she finally felt safe in her mother's arms. It was warm here. It was soft here. Nothing could hurt her now. The cannons could roar and the house could shake, but as long as she listened to her mother's heartbeat and focused on the soft caresses of her mother's hand she would be alright.

A few minutes passed. Allison even began to get a little sleepy. Then, the caresses began to slow. Then they stopped. Allison lifted up her head. "Mother?" she asked. She quickly put her head back on her mother's chest and listened. Nothing.

"Mommy?" she cried loudly. "Mommy, wake up! Don't die...not now. I need you. What can I do? Where can I go? Oh, Mommy, please don't leave me!" She hugged her mother and refused to let go. "Don't die, please don't die," she continued to sob.

Crash! Allison jumped up in fright as a cannonball smashed through the ceiling and barely missed her. It landed hard and rolled into the side of the cellar. Smoke and debris flew everywhere.

"Aaahhhh!" Allison screamed. She was almost in a total panic now. Her heart was racing, her lungs were panting, and sweat was pouring down her face. "What do I do? What do I do?" She looked around. She looked upstairs. She ran. "Daddy!" she cried as she ran.

When Allison reached the top of the stairs she froze in horror. Half of the upstairs had collapsed and had fallen on the downstairs. Beds and furniture were scattered everywhere. Paintings were lying on the floor. Her mother's jewelry case was completely smashed and the jewels were scattered all over. What remained of her bed was lying next to her toys that had all been smashed and broken. Even her doll was missing an arm. Light shone through the walls and one wall was completely destroyed. She looked outside and saw the garden marred by holes and debris. Across the street, fires from the nearby houses burned brightly. She turned and looked towards the kitchen.

"Daddy!" she called out suddenly.

Her father was pinned under pieces of the roof that had fallen. As Allison rushed towards him she could already tell that he would never walk again if he even was still alive.

"Daddy!" she called again as she approached him. "Are you alright?"

Kaboom! Another shell blasted into the house as Allison ran towards her father. This time, however, it was much closer than before. She suddenly felt a sharp pain in her head just as the explosion sent her little body flying through the air towards her father. She landed in a lump, unconscious but still breathing.

Sometime later, noises from outside woke Allison up. She had no idea whether she had been asleep for hours or even days. Her mouth was dry and she could feel an aching in her stomach that told her she had not eaten in a long time. Her head was throbbing and she felt a sharp pain in her left ear. She opened her eyes and looked up. There was screaming and yelling coming from outside.

"Yeehah!" the voices yelled. "Do it, do it, do it!"

Allison heard crashing noises as if glass and wood were being thrown around.

"Ha-ha-ha-ha-ha."

"Oh wow!"

It was laughter: laughter, yelling, and screams of joy. *What was going on?* Allison thought to herself.

She looked out the wall that was no longer there and almost fell backwards in fear and surprise at what she saw. Soldiers—Union soldiers—were dancing in the street, throwing things out of windows, drinking liquor, and even wearing women's dresses. They seemed to be crazy with joy or anger or maybe just plain drunk. Whatever it was, they were destroying the few pieces that were left of the town as they went from house to house and stole and destroyed anything they picked out.

A few of them turned towards her. Allison shrunk back. Did they see her?

Two soldiers walked right through the hole in the wall into what was left of the living room.

"What's in here, Chris?" the short, plump one said.

"I dunno, Vinny," Chris answered. He was a tall, lanky soldier with bright yellow hair and a scar on his left cheek. The two of them together looked like a sideshow of a circus. "It probably has all the same junk that's in the other houses."

"Think maybe there's anything valuable?" Vinny asked as he kicked some wood on the floor with his foot.

"I doubt it," Chris answered as he too began kicking the wood on the floor to see whether there was anything underneath. "Most of them people living here left before we started the battle. They went and took all their valuable things with them."

"Yeah, but what about that gold watch that Harry found?" Vinny said smiling. "I bet that's worth a pretty penny."

"Definitely," Chris agreed. "But I doubt we'll be so lucky as to...wait a minute. What's this?"

Allison shrunk back in fear, afraid that the men had seen her.

"It looks like jewels," Vinny said as he saw what Chris had found.

Oh no! Allison thought to herself. *They've found Mommy's jewelry.*

"Whew," Chris whistled. "I bet this stuff's worth a lot."

"Let's see what else there is," Vinny said enthusiastically, as a look of pleasure and greed appeared on his face.

"Hey, check this out," Vinny called. "Looks like a family portrait or something. Think it's worth anything?"

"Nahh," Chris answered as he took the bayonet from his rifle and slashed through the portrait. "I bet it's just a picture of some locals. Maybe even the people who lived here."

Our portrait! Allison cried out to herself as she watched the bayonet rip through her father's face in the portrait.

"Hey, check out this clock," Vinny called again.

"What are you gonna do with a clock?" Chris asked doubtfully.

"I dunno," Vinny replied. "Maybe I can give it to the captain and we can use it instead of reveille."

"Heh, heh," Chris chuckled. "C'mon, you idiot. Let's hurry up and finish. The colonel's bound to stop all this fun any minute."

"Yeah, O.K.," Vinny agreed as he threw the clock against the wall and watched it smash into tiny pieces.

The men continued to search through the debris for more items to steal as Allison looked on helplessly. She wanted to scream at them, but she knew that if they saw her they might hurt her or even kill her with the sharp bayonets on the ends of their rifles.

"Hey, Vinny," Chris called after a few minutes. "Look at the little dolly."

"Heh, heh," Vinny laughed as he saw Chris holding the doll by its one remaining arm.

"Pretty ugly, ain't it?" Chris laughed.

"Yeah," Vinny agreed. "Kinda reminds me of the rest of the rebs. Ugly, tattered, and weak."

"And tomorrow we'll do this to them!" Chris laughed as he tore the other arm off the doll and tossed it on the floor. "C'mon. Let's get outta here."

CHAPTER TEN
THE SLAUGHTER

Finally, finally, I'm gonna see some action, George said to himself as he watched the Union soldiers gathering at the edge of the city.

George had been bivouacked with his regiment at Fredericksburg for four weeks and he was tired of waiting, watching, and working. When they first arrived, they found the Federal army already camped on the other side of the Rappahannock River. The Yankees appeared to be gathering strength and preparing to cross into Fredericksburg. Upon seeing this, General Lee, the overall Southern commander, had ordered General Longstreet, who commanded over 35,000 men, to take a position on the high ground behind the city. Since George's regiment was commanded by Major General Pickett, who was under Longstreet's command, George was part of this force.

As soon as they arrived, George could tell that they were in a good position. They were on the top of Marye's Heights and could see the entire city. It reminded George of the previous year's rock fight against the Fifth Street Cats when his gang sat in a protective position at the top of the hill and fired down at the poor boys scrambling for cover.

Of course the soldiers did not rely solely on the hill to provide them with cover. Fences and stone walls

along the heights provided some protection. One por-
tion of the road along the heights was a little lower
than the surrounding area and was lined by a stone
wall. The men began to call this area the sunken road
since it would hide them from view and, at the same
time, enable them to reload and fire down at the oncoming Federals.

The next three weeks were spent doing what most
armies did: watching, waiting, and doing chores. General Lee had already decided that since the Federals
outnumbered them, they would lie and wait in their
well-defended positions to destroy the enemy as they
marched up the hills. In preparation, they dug trenches
and looked for firewood. They cut down long branches
and made huge spears, which were placed in front of
their fortifications. They sang songs and practiced load-
ing and reloading their guns. They drilled. They
marched. They played cards and they prayed.

Two days later, the Federals finally made their
move. Engineers from the Union arrived and began
building bridges to cross the river. But General
Longstreet would not let them cross into the city so
easily. He ordered General Barksdale to bring his Mississippi men to the opposite side of the river and fire
on the bridge builders from the protection of the city
itself. Every time the Federals tried to build their bridge,
they were fired upon by the Confederates who hid in
the buildings. In response, General Burnside, the Federal commander, had ordered his cannons to open fire
upon the city in an attempt to dislodge the Confederate sharpshooters.

George watched in horror as the Federal cannons
began an attack on the city. Everywhere he looked, cannonballs tore wide holes in houses, uprooted trees, dug
craters in yards and gardens, and sent debris flying
everywhere. Fires began to burn as huge columns of
dark, dense smoke rose into the air. Once in a while,

George would see a few civilians running for cover. *At least, George thought, most of them had evacuated the city before the firing began.*

By the end of the day, the Federals had managed to cross the river in boats, and General Longstreet eventually ordered the Mississippi men to pull back. He would not fight in the city but would wait for the Federals to attack them in their position along the heights.

The next day was even worse for George. Waiting for the Federal army to advance, George stood helplessly as he watched the Union soldiers ransack the town. They broke what store windows remained, ran into houses to steal jewelry, money, and other items of value. They ran up and down the streets drinking, singing, smashing, and stealing. They grabbed children's toys and wore women's dresses. They chased pigs and chickens down the streets. It was the most heartless, cruel craziness that George had ever seen.

Now, George would finally get his chance to pay back those soldiers for what they did to the city. As the morning fog slowly lifted, he could see the Federal troops gathering in the streets and heading their way. George flinched as the sudden thunder of the Southern cannons behind him opened up and fired at the Federal's advance.

"When are we gonna move up?" George shouted to Eric over the noise. The two had been standing at each other's side throughout the week.

"We aren't," Eric said bitterly.

"What?" George said in surprise.

"We're to be held in reserve," Eric explained. "It seems that Ransom's boys get to have all the fun."

George's shoulders slumped and his face fell as his eyes turned slowly towards the battle. *When, dear Lord,* he prayed to himself, *will I get a chance to prove myself?*

The mass of blue uniforms moved steadily up the hill as the bayonets on their rifles glistened in the sun. Hundreds of men formed into lines that stretched over the entire width of the fields. They moved with such determination and power that it seemed as if they would march right through the Confederates lying in wait. Cannonballs exploded in the Union soldiers' midst, landing on their heads and smashing through their bodies. Each shot struck 9 or 10 men at a time, creating huge gaps in their lines. But the holes were quickly filled by other men as the mass of Union soldiers continued up the hill.

The Federals continued to progress and were almost within one hundred feet of the stone wall where the Confederate soldiers had dug in. George watched with fear as he realized that the boys in blue were getting too close. Suddenly, with a roar of thunder and a burst of flames, the Confederates fired an intense volley of rifle fire bullets that wiped out almost the entire front line of the Federals. More volleys of Minié balls quickly followed as hundreds of men fell screaming to the ground. Faces were splattered, stomachs shot clean through, legs shattered, and arms blown off. The Confederates continued to fire repeatedly as the Union soldiers staggered backwards, trying to reload and fire amidst the rain of metal. Within 20 minutes, the men in blue had either retreated to some temporary cover or ran away completely, leaving their dead and dying comrades behind on the field.

"Yeee-hah!" George cried out as he waved his hat. "That'll show them Yankees not to mess with us."

As George continued to look on, hoping and praying for a chance to fight, and with his hands gripping his rifle tighter and tighter each passing minute, the men in blue advanced again. They almost made it to the top and even managed to hold steady for an instant, but the rifle fire was too intense and they were forced to retreat. Another line of soldiers came and then another, each one facing the same terrible slaughter.

"How do they keep it up?" Eric said at one point.

"I don't know," Bruce commented. He had been standing near Eric and George for most of the battle. "But you sure gotta respect the way those boys keep trying."

"I guess so," Eric agreed.

"Seems kind of stupid to me," George added.

"That's cuz they aren't making it through," Bruce replied. "If they do make it through somehow, we'll all be singing a different tune."

"Yeah maybe," Eric agreed again. "Hey, George," he said suddenly, turning his head towards a new regiment of Union soldiers climbing up the hill. "You see that flag?"

"Which one?" George asked.

"The green one," Eric pointed out. "Right in the middle of those soldiers with the green in their hats."

"Oh yeah," George answered as his eyes caught the emerald green flag rushing up the hill. "That must be an Irish regiment. See the shamrocks?"

"Yeah, that's what I thought," Eric replied. He was Irish like George, although his family had come to America much earlier. "Too bad they've got to be in this."

"Yeah," George mumbled. His thoughts drifted to his Irish friends in Boston and the times they spent playing baseball and running through the Irish slums in the city. "I wonder if any of them are from Boston?"

Eric didn't answer as he and George watched the Irish regiment suffer the same fate as the others before them. It seemed to George that they stood a little longer and got a little closer to the wall but like all the others, they were forced to retreat.

The battle dragged into the afternoon, and George was beginning to think his regiment would never be called on to fight. His feelings varied from disappointment, because he was not participating in the battle, to relief that he would not have to be responsible for the slaughter of so many soldiers. After all, George remembered, he used to live in the North and he might even know some of those boys who were dying on the fields. At one point, when the Irish were marching up the hill, he even thought he saw John O'Malley, the leader of the slum gang back in Boston.

Sometime during the early afternoon, the order finally came. George and the men in his company were told to join the others who were in the sunken road firing on the Federal troops. Excitement spread through the boys, their hearts beat fast with anticipation, and their hands began to sweat. They quickly moved over to their position on the road, keeping their heads down to avoid the few shots from the Union soldiers.

Within several minutes they had formed a line, 5 or 6 deep, behind the stone wall. George was amazed at how perfect the wall was. As he stood against it, he could see everything down the field, but the stones were placed so tightly together and at the perfect height, that he could hold out his rifle, take aim, and only expose his head and shoulders.

He double-checked his rifle to make sure it was loaded. He did not want to miss his opportunity to fire. Although George could load his gun fairly quickly after each shot, he could only fire when it was his turn since the men rotated through the lines as they fired. One group would fire at the Union soldiers then stand back to reload while the next group advanced and fired. This ensured that a constant rain of bullets fell on the enemy, but only if George and the others could reload their rifles in the short time they had between turns.

As another regiment of Federals marched up the hill, George and the others watched and waited. The boys in blue fired at them and George watched as a few of his comrades fell to the ground after being hit by some of the Federal Minié balls that had made their way over the wall. Still, the Confederates held their fire, and the boys in blue continued to advance.

"Fire!"

George pressed the trigger and felt the gun push back against his shoulder as the rifle discharged. Smoke from all of the guns rose into the air. George struggled to see through it, but was thrown backwards by the hand of the soldier behind him.

"Reload, you idiot!" the soldier barked at him as he took George's spot at the wall.

George staggered backwards and absentmindedly reached for another cartridge from his sack. It was a good thing he had drilled this so many times, over and over, day after day, because his mind was so caught up in watching the Federals continue to advance that his concentration was not at its best. His hands stumbled over his rifle and shook as he continued opening his cartridge bag, stuffing the ramrod in the rifle, and preparing the spark. Another volley sang out at the Federals followed by another and another. Again, heads snapped back, blood spurted into the air, limbs were shot off, and bodies were pierced as the Union soldiers died by the hundreds until they broke off and ran.

The Union soldiers tried two or three more times before they finally gave up. One regiment tried running up the hill over the bodies of their comrades with their bayonets fixed without even stopping to fire. They actually made it a little farther than the others, but they too were shot once they got close enough to the wall. By the end of the battle, thousands of Union soldiers lay on the grass in front of George, not one of whom had ever made it close enough to even touch the stone wall. The battle was over.

DEAD CONFEDERATES LAY BEHIND THE STONE WALL

CHAPTER ELEVEN
HELL'S ANGEL

Two days later George was still upset at what he had seen. He couldn't believe what the Union soldiers had done: running up like that, row after row of them only to be slaughtered as easily as one would cut down blades of grass with a scythe. Even worse was that he had actually done some of the killing.

It was the first time he had killed someone. Before, as a drummer boy, he only had been able to watch the actual battles, even at Antietam when so many men had fallen. He had watched with envy as the boys who were older or bigger than he got involved in the fighting and actually made a difference. George had begged for a chance to fight, to show his worth, and to make a difference.

Now that he actually had been given that chance he was having a hard time dealing with it. It was nothing like he had expected. At first it was exciting and scary. His heart pumped with adrenaline; his body shook with energy; and he felt like he could conquer the world. But after it all was over, the gruesome images of the soldiers dying from their limbs flying in the air or from their faces being shot off continued to run through his mind.

My God, George thought to himself as he sat with his friends under the stars and listened to the groans of the men still dying slowly on the battlefield. Although the fighting seemed to cease for the moment, neither side had been able to go out in front of the stone wall to remove the dead or wounded for fear of being shot. It had created an eerie, unreal feeling as if he were in some strange nightmare just waiting for something terrible to happen. He inhaled another breath of the cool night air as some soldier wailed an agonizing cry for water.

My God, he repeated in his mind, *what have I done? Did I really help to kill all of those men? Was it my shot that tore off that man's head or ripped off another's leg? Are any of those men dying out there holding one of my bullets in their body? And if they die, does that make me a murderer? No, of course not,* George thought to himself immediately. He shook his head back and forth in reaction to his own harsh thoughts. *This is war. You're supposed to kill in war. It's part of life. They attack us, we attack them. Look at what they did to Fredericksburg after all. They had it coming. They deserved what we did to them. Every last one of them. But,* his thoughts continued, *still, I can't believe God would sit back and let us viciously kill each other. Doesn't he care? Doesn't he love us? Father always said he did. Even when mother died he said that God would take care of her because he loves all of us. Maybe we did something wrong. Maybe he is punishing us for something. Maybe it's like Noah's ark all over again, instead of rain he's sending bullets. Naahh, that's stupid. This ain't no Bible story and I ain't no Noah, that's for sure. I bet God just doesn't care. Or maybe he wants us to fight. Or maybe he isn't there at all.*

"Ahhhh, the heck with it!" George said out loud as he stood up in frustration.

"The heck with what?" Eric cried as his head shot back in confusion. The two of them had been sitting quietly under the night sky for several hours and George's sudden outburst startled Eric.

"Nothing," George mumbled. "I was just thinking about all these dead guys."

"It's the guys that are still alive that I don't like," Eric said. "Crying for water, screaming in pain, sobbing out of control. It's enough to drive you crazy."

"Sure is," George answered. "Makes you want to run away."

Pow, pow, pow! Shots suddenly rang through the air. Eric and George instinctively ducked.

"What's going on?" Eric shouted as he and George stood up and turned towards the noise.

"That's coming from the Union soldiers," George responded as his eyes peered into the darkness to try to see what was happening.

"Think they're gonna try another attack?" Eric wondered aloud.

"They'd be crazy to," George answered. "They wouldn't get any further than they did before."

"Then what do you think's going on?" Eric asked.

"I dunno," George answered with a shrug of his shoulders. "Wait, look!"

Eric looked to where George was pointing. Over the stone wall, amidst the bodies of hundreds of Union soldiers, was a Confederate soldier wandering amongst them with as many canteens of water as he could carry.

"What's he doing?" Eric wondered.

"It looks like he's trying to give water to all those soldiers," George answered slowly.

"I thought we weren't supposed to cross the line," Eric said.

"We're not," George answered.

"He's gonna get himself killed," Eric said in an angry tone. "The stupid idiot."

"He's not stupid," George disagreed. "Just brave."

The gunshots finally stopped as the Union soldiers realized that the soldier was helping their wounded comrades. Both sides continued to watch as the man walked from soldier to soldier, checking to see whether they were alive and giving those who were some water from his canteens.

"Give me your canteen," George ordered suddenly.

"What?" Eric asked in a confused tone. "Why?"

"I'm gonna give it to that soldier so he can help more men," George answered. "We may be ordered to not let anyone else cross the line, but that doesn't mean we can't help him."

"Here," Eric responded eagerly as he took the canteen and handed it to George. "See that he gets it."

George smiled, grabbed the canteen, and made his way along the stone wall to where he could reach the soldier. *Finally he was doing something good,* George thought. *So what if the men were Union soldiers. They were still human beings and he wasn't about to watch them suffer when he could do something about it. Besides, he would certainly want them to do the same for him.*

Cheers erupted from both sides of the lines as the man returned to get more canteens.

"Excuse me, excuse me," George said as he made his way through his fellow soldiers along the road. "Here, here," he said panting as he handed the canteens to the soldier. "Use these too."

"Thanks," the soldier said with a smile.

"Were you ordered to do this?" George asked of the man.

"No," the man replied. "I asked General Kershaw for permission and he gave it."

"What's your name?" another soldier asked as he too handed him a canteen.

"Kirkland...Sergeant Richard Kirkland, 2nd South Carolina,"[1] the man answered as he turned to take more water to the Union soldiers.

---

1. Sergeant Richard Rowland Kirkland, 19 years old, actually volunteered on this errand of mercy according to the records of General J. B. Kershaw. Today, the Angel of Marye's Heights monument stands in honor of Sergeant Kirkland in Fredericksburg, Virginia.

"God bless you then, Kirkland," the soldier shouted.

"God bless you," George and the other 10 or 20 soldiers around him repeated.

George made his way back to his position with Eric and watched as Sergeant Kirkland continued his mission of mercy. For over an hour he made his way around the bodies, sometimes stumbling over a group of dead men who lay so close together there was no place to put his foot down. Each time he found a man alive, he would give him water and move on to the next.

"At least if they die," George said aloud as he watched Kirkland return to the Confederate side amidst a chorus of cheers, "they'll die a little more comfortably."

Chapter Twelve
Snowballs

"Guys, look at this, look at this!" George shouted as he held a newspaper in one hand and ran into the group of soldiers who were huddled around the campfire. It was another bitter, cold January day, and the boys were trying to keep warm after finishing their various chores. Since the excitement of that week in December, boredom had taken its hold on the soldiers as they waited for another day of battle. The battle of Fredericksburg appeared to be over and the Union had lost yet again. General Burnside, the Union commander, had ordered his troops to retreat to the other side of the Rappahannock River after the disaster at Marye's Heights. Then, both armies settled down to watch each other and wait for the next fight.

"What is it, George?" Bruce asked from his crouched position. His hands finally had begun to warm up enough so that he could move his fingers again, and he wasn't about to get up for anyone.

"Them Northerners are just as angry at Lincoln as we are," George claimed as he held up the newspaper in his hands.

"About what?" Eric asked.

"They're calling him an incompetent president who can't run a war," George explained as he opened the paper in his hands for all to see. "And even better is that there are all kinds of people complaining about the Emancipation Proclamation."

"You mean the one freeing the slaves?" Eric asked.

"Yeah," George replied, crouching down and taking a position in between Eric and Bruce. He stuck the newspaper under his armpit, rubbed his hands together, and then held them out to the fire. "I just read an editorial in the New York paper about it. I tried to get a Philadelphia paper, but this was the only one I could trade for."

"You traded your tobacco for a newspaper?" Mike wondered aloud. He knew that trade between the Federal soldiers and the Confederates across the river was a regular occurrence and he himself had traded with them once or twice. Still, he couldn't imagine why George would waste his time and tobacco on a newspaper, especially a Northern one. "Why didn't you get more food?"

"I wanted to get a Philadelphia paper to see if there was any news about my relatives," George answered.

"You mean your uncle?" Eric asked from George's right.

"And my cousins," George added. "They're the ones I really miss. We used to write letters to each other all the time, but ever since the war started we've lost touch. I think they may have even signed up with the Union army. They were talking about it in their last letter."

"So what are they saying about Lincoln?" Bruce interrupted.

"Who?" George asked in confusion.

"The Northern papers!" Bruce exclaimed.

"Oh yeah, right," George said in an embarrassed tone. He removed the paper from under his arm and held it up again. "They're saying that if Lincoln is gonna free the slaves, then why don't he free all the slaves? He only freed them in the South but not in the border states."

"He can't free our slaves!" Bobby interrupted.

"Of course he can't," Russell explained from the other side of the fire. He had taken off his glasses and was trying to clean them with a handkerchief. It seemed that his glasses were always fogging up in this bitter cold. "But he thinks he can. That is, he believes that we are still part of the United States, which means that he can still pass laws to control us."

"That's ridiculous," Bobby exclaimed.

"That's exactly what this paper is saying," George went on. "They are saying that all the Emancipation Proclamation is gonna do is make Union soldiers desert cuz they ain't gonna fight a war to free our slaves."

"Good, that'll get us home that much sooner," Bobby said simply. It was clear he had no real interest in the news, especially from up North.

"Does the paper say anything else interesting," Russell asked as he put his glasses back on while Bobby gave him a glare.

"Well, let's see," George said as he stood up and opened the paper completely. "There's something here about the draft and about the Federals getting black people to fight now and...hey!"

George's newspaper collapsed in his hands as something smashed right into it. "What the...," George yelled.

The boys all turned to see what had been thrown at George when 15-20 small snowballs suddenly came flying into their group.

"Snowball fight!" someone screamed as they all stood up and began to grab the snow with their hands. The snow was extremely cold, especially to their fire-warmed hands, which made it difficult at first to form the snow into a ball.

"Spread out, take cover!" Kevin yelled. Even though he was a private like the rest of the boys, Kevin's experiences back home in Richmond as the gang leader of the Fifth Street Cats had made him used to giving orders. Even Bobby and Bruce, the leaders of George's old gang, listened to him.

The boys all ran for trees and bushes where they could make their snowballs without getting hit immediately. George was hit four times in the back and once in the head as he ducked and darted from left to right.

"How did they throw so many snowballs so quickly?" George yelled to Eric as he picked up his hat off the ground.

"They're forming an infantry line just like we do in drills!" Eric explained. He glanced back at the oncoming soldiers and recognized the formation. "While one group is throwing, the other group is behind them making their snowballs."

"They must have planned this," George determined as he finally reached a large bush that both he and Eric could hide behind. "There's no way that they could have organized so quickly. Who is it, the 3rd?"

"Nah, it's them South Carolina boys," Eric corrected. "They've been angry at us ever since you made that wisecrack about Charleston."

"I didn't mean it the way it sounded," George tried to explain.

"I know," Eric agreed. "But they don't. Now hurry up and start making some snowballs."

George reached down, made another snowball, and placed it next to Eric.

"Great," Eric said gleefully, "we're just like the artillery boys. You supply the ammo and I'll do the firing. Keep up the good work. They seem to be falling back."

The snowball fight was becoming larger as news of it spread throughout the Army of Northern Virginia. Boys from the Virginia regiments had come in to reinforce George's unit. Other soldiers from Texas and Georgia had joined the opposition.

"It's becoming everyone against Virginia!" George cried.

"I'm gonna try to make it across the field to Bobby," Eric said suddenly. "You cover me."

"But," George argued as Eric darted out from the bush cover. Instantly, a mass of snowballs descended on Eric. He fell backwards a few steps.

"Cover me!" he yelled back to George.

"I am," George said laughing, "I am."

George hurled as many of the snowballs as he could at the other boys. Three or four balls hit and stopped the boys for a second, but it made no difference. Eric was bombarded from all sides by snowballs. They hit him in the legs, the stomach, the head, and on the butt. George couldn't help but laugh.

"Stop, stop!" Eric cried out, waving his hands as he stood.

Ten, twenty, thirty snowballs all fell upon Eric as he collapsed in a heap. A cheer sounded from the other side while Eric lay on his back in the snow.

"We ain't giving up yet!" George heard Bobby yell. "Fire!"

Snowballs from George's side of the field blasted the enemy. The boys staggered and started to fall back but not before 3 of them grabbed Eric by the feet and dragged him towards their barricade.

"We got ourselves a prisoner," they said laughing.

"George, help!" Eric screamed as he was being dragged. He arched his neck and looked back towards George. "Don't let these awful boys take me. Save me! Save meeeee!"

George laughed at Eric's antics. *I suppose I should help him. Besides, it will be fun sneaking behind enemy lines,* George thought to himself.

George walked slowly at first with his head lowered so the enemy could not see or hear his movements. He turned deeper into the woods. The best way for him to help Eric would be to swing out a little into the woods and then surprise the South Carolinians from behind. Realizing that the snow was hiding a lot of the noise of his movements, George increased his pace. *If only his feet weren't so cold*, he thought.

George heard a noise ahead. He stopped suddenly. Was another soldier out here too?

Crack, a twig snapped and a figure moved.

"Gotcha!" George yelled as he hit the figure in the head with a snowball.

Whoever it was must have been surprised because he fell down almost immediately. George rushed forward.

"Uhhh, ah-uh, ah-uh."

George stopped and listened.

The person was crying! What kind of timid soldier was this? George thought.

"Hey, don't cry," George said in an annoyed tone as he approached the figure. "It was only a snowball."

George knelt beside him. He was too small to be a soldier. *Perhaps a drummer boy*, George thought.

"I said don't cry," George repeated out loud as he turned the person over from its crouched position.

"Huh?" George exclaimed falling backwards in surprise as he stared open-mouthed at the small girl slowly backing away from him. She was clothed in what appeared to be a dress, but it was so torn and tattered that her skin showed through it, and her body vibrated noticeably in the cold.

"You're a girl?" George said slowly.

She said nothing. George knew by the look of terror on her face and in her deep blue eyes that she was no ordinary girl.

"Calm down, calm down," George said softly, as she began to back away. "I ain't gonna hurt you."

The girl continued to back away.

"Stop," George commanded. "I only want to talk to you."

The girl turned and started to run.

"Stop!" George yelled again as he ran after her.

The girl turned, darted through a bush, then ran around a tree. George followed her as fast as he could, but he was unable to keep up with her despite his superior size.

"Where'd she go?" George asked out loud as he stopped and looked around in every direction. "She sure is quick for a little girl."

Snap!

George flung his head around at the sound of the breaking twig.

"Wait!" he called out again.

The girl continued to run through bushes and under tree limbs trying to get away, but George was determined to catch her. Instead of running full speed and losing her around a corner, this time he stayed back a little, kept an eye on her, and waited for his chance to spring.

"Gotcha!" he yelled as he jumped forward and tackled her. The force pushed them both into the deep snow. George had trouble sitting upright, but he made sure not to let go of the girl.

"Stop squirming!" he yelled as she twisted and turned and pulled at him.

"I said stop squirming!" George repeated as he grabbed her with his other arm as well.

The girl slapped him suddenly in the face either in anger or in fright.

"Ow," George yelled as he returned the slap. "That hurt!"

The girl began to sob.

"Hey, don't cry," George said quickly. "I didn't mean to hurt you. You just surprised me, that's all."

The girl continued to cry.

"Didn't you hear me?" George asked. "I said I ain't gonna hurt you."

The girl continued to cry.

"Hey," George said as he gently grabbed her chin and turned her face towards him, "I said stop...huh?"

George stared at the girl's face in shock as she continued to cry. He hadn't noticed it before, especially from far away, but it looked as if there was dried blood on the side of her head.

What's going on here? George wondered as he stared more carefully at the girl. He reached for her hair. She backed away.

"I ain't gonna hurt you," he said slowly as he moved her hair back away from her right cheek.

"Ohhhh," George groaned as he saw a large amount of flesh amassed on the side of her head. "Your ear has been shot clean off. No wonder you didn't listen to me."

The girl shied away again. George turned his voice towards her ear on the left side. "I ain't gonna hurt you," he repeated in as gentle a voice as he could. "In fact, I wanna help you."

The girl looked up at him quizzically but did not react.

At least she ain't trying to run away again, George thought to himself.

"You must be hungry!" George thought suddenly as he reached into his pocket and pulled out a half-eaten piece of hardtack and handed it to her.

The girl looked at him nervously, looked down at the hardtack, back at George, then grabbed the piece suddenly and shoved it in her mouth.

"Boy you sure are hungry," George said as he watched her chew the stale, rocklike piece of bread.

The girl looked up at him when she was done. George noticed how beautiful her eyes were and how full and blond her hair was. Despite the rags on her body, the blood on her face, and the smoke and dirt in her hair, she was quite pretty. "What have the Yankees done to you?" George asked out loud.

The girl turned suddenly at the mention of the Yankees, and George could tell that something terrible must have happened to her. He stood up and tried to quickly change the subject.

"There's more food back at camp," he said loudly in the direction of her left side. "Why don't you come with me?"

The girl looked at George's outstretched hand and backed away.

"Please, I only want to help you," George begged.

The girl looked up again, then down at the ground. George followed her eyes. It was the first time he had noticed the small armless doll in her hands. George suddenly remembered his little cousin Helen playing with her own doll in the apartment back at Boston. It had always amazed him how girls played with dolls and sometimes even treated them like little people.

"Maybe we can even fix your friend too!" he said enthusiastically.

The girl looked up again then back down at her doll.

George waited patiently with his hand still outstretched. He didn't dare move.

Finally, slowly, the girl reached up her hand and held George's.

"Alright!" George cried. "Let's go get some food."

CHAPTER THIRTEEN
INTRODUCTIONS

"Hey guys, look what I found," George called as he led the younger girl by the hand and approached the gang huddled around the fire. The snowball fight had long since ended and even Eric was back in his usual spot, crouching down with his palms held out towards the flames.

"What?" several of the boys called as they turned their heads.

"Hey," one boy said.

"A girl?" said another.

All the boys turned in surprise to look at the person who George had brought into the camp. It wasn't the long blond hair or bright blue eyes that surprised them. They had seen girls before. It wasn't even her small bare feet that barely left footprints in the snow. They had seen many children wandering around looking for their parents. It was probably that it was so late and she was so alone. By now most of the homeless kids had been placed in makeshift aid stations like churches and schools where they could be cared for by volunteers.

"Where'd you find her?" Russell asked as George brought the girl into the middle of the group. She was reluctant at first and very nervous around so many soldiers, but she seemed O.K. as long as George stayed

107

close. She squeezed his hand tighter and the feeling somehow comforted George.

"She was hiding in the woods," George began. "During the fight I had snuck around to try to catch the South Carolinians by surprise so I could free Eric but—"

"So that's where you went!" Steven commented. "I was wondering where you disappeared to."

"Yeah," Eric added, "I was waiting forever to be rescued! What happened?"

"He was telling you," Russell scolded. "If you hadn't interrupted we'd have heard by now."

"I didn't interrupt," Eric snapped back.

"You did too."

"No, I didn't," Eric repeated. "It was Steven who—"

"Will you guys shut up!" Bobby yelled as he waved his hands. "I wanna hear what George has to say."

Eric and Russell looked down at the ground in silence.

"Go ahead, George," Bobby said softly once everyone was quiet.

"Anyway," George began. His voice started off slow, but as he discussed what happened he talked faster and faster, rushing to get to the end. "I was going through the woods trying to get around the South Carolinians when I heard this noise in the bushes. I thought it was another soldier, so I threw a snowball, but it turned out to be this girl. She was crying and ran away from me, but I caught her and gave her some hardtack to eat. She ate it so fast that I thought I should bring her here for some more."

"What's her name?" Bobby asked.

"I don't know," George replied awkwardly. "I never asked her."

"Where's her family?" Bobby continued.

"Uh...I don't know that either."

"Is she from Fredericksburg?"

George looked down at his feet. He felt stupid.

"What *do* you know about her?" Bobby asked in a huff.

"Nothing," George admitted. "All I know is that she's hungry."

"Well here," Steven said as he reached into his haversack and pulled out some more hardtack, "give her some of this."

"Yeah, I got some too," Bobby added.

The boys all began reaching into their haversacks or pockets or looking around to find some food for the little girl. Unfortunately, there wasn't much to go around. Supplies everywhere were already low, and General Lee had even ordered a cutback on food throughout the army.

"Look at her go," Steven commented as he watched her shove piece after piece of hardtack into her mouth. "She must not have eaten in days."

"Or maybe even weeks," Eric added. "We've been here a long time."

"A body can't go that long without food," Bobby argued.

"It can if you get water," Russell responded.

"Where's she gonna get water?" Jason asked quickly.

"Lotsa places," Eric answered. "She could even eat the snow."

"Look at her feet," someone else commented.

"Must be frostbite," Steven replied as he and the others stared at her black and green toes. The skin looked parched and dry even though they had been in the wet snow for so long.

"She needs shoes," Eric mumbled.

"Of course she needs shoes," Bobby said angrily. "A lot of us need shoes, socks, a shirt, a cap, gloves, or a half-decent meal. But we ain't got none of that so what are we gonna do for her?"

"She can have my socks," George said simply.

"Your new socks?" Eric exclaimed. "The ones your mom made for you?"

"Stepmom," George corrected.

"Whatever!" Eric said angrily. "You can't give up them socks. They was made just for you and you ain't got nothin' else."

"I still got my shoes," George said simply.

The boys all watched as George bent down and reached for his shoes.

"Don't worry," George said softly to the girl. She had become nervous when George had let go of her hand and was trying to grab it back. "I ain't going nowhere."

George sat near the fire and began to untie his shoes while everyone else looked on. Once the shoes were taken off he laid them to the side and removed his socks. The air felt bitter on his toes and he quickly rubbed his feet with his hands.

"I can't believe some of you guys have been going barefoot all this time," George commented as he slipped his shoes back on his bare feet. The shoes were cold and the leather scratched his toes uncomfortably.

"C'mere," George said as he reached his hand out to the girl. "I've got something for you."

She held his outstretched hand and let George pull her down next to him.

"She likes you, George," Eric noticed.

"Nahhh," George argued half-heartedly. "She just likes all the stuff I've been givin' her. Is that better?" he asked her as he slipped the socks onto her feet.

She smiled and nodded her head up and down.

"Those ain't gonna do much once they get wet in the snow," Russell said.

"I know," George agreed, "but at least it'll help for a little while."

"What's your name, little girl?" Steven asked suddenly as he bent down near her.

"She ain't gonna hear you," George informed him. "Her ear has been shot off on that side."

Steven stared at the girl's head and gently lifted her hair back.

"Ohhhh," he and several other soldiers groaned.

"Damn Yankees," a few boys said.

"Try the other side," George suggested.

Steven rose and came around to the girl's left side.

"What's your name?" he asked again.

She didn't answer.

"What's your name?" Steven repeated a little louder.

"She's deaf in that ear too!" Eric yelled.

"No, she ain't," Bobby argued. "Hey girl, here's some more food!" Bobby called from a little farther away and off to the side.

"See her turn her head?" Bobby pointed out. "She can hear fine. She either don't wanna answer or she can't answer."

"Maybe she forgot," Eric suggested.

"What?" Steven cried, making fun of Eric. "How can you forget your own name?"

"It happens," Russell answered as Steven glared at him. "I've heard of people who have been in a battle or in some terrible place during the war and they forgot their name and where they lived and everything."

"You think that's what happened to her?" Eric asked.

"I dunno," Russell answered.

"What are we gonna do then?" Eric asked again.

"Watch," Bobby interrupted. "I know how to find out her name."

Bobby turned and walked until he was just behind the girl on her left side and sat down quietly.

"Mary," he called in a soft, gentle voice. The girl continued staring into the fire and rubbing her toes as if she couldn't hear a thing.

"Sallie," he called again in the same soft voice.

"What's he doing?" Eric asked to no one in particular.

"He's seeing if she'll react to a name," Steven said with a smile. "What a great idea!"

Steven quickly stood up and moved quietly next to Bobby.

"Rachel," he called. "Helen...Joanne...Leslie."

The boys were beginning to get frustrated.

"Ruth...Heidi."

Still nothing.

"This is crazy," Jason complained as he threw a snowball into the fire and watched the sparks fly. "She's never gonna do nothin'."

"Allison."

The girl turned her head a little.

"That's it!" Jason cried as he turned back towards the others and watched in surprise.

"Allison?" George called gently but loud enough that she could easily hear him. She turned her head completely and looked at George.

"Allison?" he said again. The girl nodded.

"Yee-hah!" the boys yelled and clapped. Allison jumped back a little.

"Don't be afraid," George said with a laugh. "They're just happy."

Allison smiled a little and looked around.

"What now?" Eric asked.

"Ask her where her parents are!" Steven suggested to George.

"Where are your parents?" George said softly.

Allison just looked down at the ground. Everyone grew quiet. They all knew what Allison's bowed head meant. They had seen it too much this past month.

"Are you from Fredericksburg?" George asked after another moment or two.

Allison did not move.

"Allison," George called a little sterner this time. She looked up at him. "Are you from Fredericksburg?"

She nodded her head yes.

"Do you have any relatives or friends still left in the town?" George asked.

Allison shrugged her shoulders.

"You better get her to an aid station," Russell interrupted. "They can help her."

"But it's almost dark," Eric added. "He'll never make it back before curfew."

"She can't sleep here," Russell said.

"Why not?" Bobby asked. "It's not like she's a Yankee spy or something."

"You know the rules," Russell reminded him. "You want us all to get into trouble?"

"No one's gonna get in trouble," Steven interrupted. "Because no one's gonna tell. Right, guys?"

Steven looked around the fire as all the boys shook their heads, even Russell, although not right away.

"Plus," Bobby added, "what are they gonna say? That we should've sent the poor girl on her way in the dark and the cold?"

"Alright," Russell agreed, "but where is she gonna sleep?"

"With George," Bobby answered simply.

"Me?" George said quickly. "Why me?"

"Cuz you found her, dummy," Steven answered before Bobby could. "Besides, she obviously likes you and if any of us try to take her she'd just cry anyway."

"But," George protested.

"No buts," Steven said firmly, holding up his hand. "The girl will sleep with you. In the morning you'll take her to an aid station while we cover for you and get your chores done. Understand?"

George looked around. Everyone seemed to agree with Steven as they nodded approvingly and looked at George in anticipation.

"Yeah, O.K.," George finally agreed. "I'll take care of her."

CHAPTER FOURTEEN
REFUGEES

The walk to the nearest aid station was several miles. George had to wake especially early to make sure he would be back in time for dinner. First, he made sure that the army would not be moving out that day. Then he told Eric he was on his way.

"Good luck," Eric whispered to both George and Allison who were standing in the tent holding hands. Allison was still holding her armless doll in one hand and staring blankly across the tent. Her eyes seemed to hide all kinds of sad thoughts that Eric could only begin to guess at. She still hadn't said a word since her arrival yesterday.

"I hope you find someone to take care of you," Eric said to Allison as she followed George out the tent.

"Bye," George called, stepping out into the cold morning air. He looked around and noticed that the sun had not yet completely risen and for a moment George watched as his breath formed clouds in the air. Then the wind blew on his face and up his shirt. It felt as if cold needles were being pushed into his skin all over. He began to shiver almost uncontrollably. Buttoning his jacket made him a little warmer, but his feet were especially cold now that he no longer was wearing any socks. Within a few steps, the cold, damp snow started to leak into his shoes, and he began wondering why he had been so nice to give away his socks in the first place.

He looked at Allison. She was shivering too. Her little hand was still holding George's and George could feel the shaking all the way up to his shoulders. He looked down at Allison's feet and realized that the socks were already soaking wet from the snow. He felt ashamed that he had second thoughts about giving her the socks. He took off his jacket and draped it over her shoulders.

"Would you like my shoes?" George added as he stopped walking and pointed down at his feet. "They'll keep you a lot warmer."

Allison looked down at her feet then over at George's and smiled.

George was confused. What was she smiling about? He looked at his feet and hers again, then he smiled too.

"I get it," he said with a slight grin. "Your feet would never fit in my shoes, would they?"

Allison grinned slightly and shook her head. George felt a little silly.

"Oh well," he said, turning back towards the road and continuing on. "Guess we'll just need to hurry then."

Perhaps the only good thing about the freezing cold is that once you go numb the pain goes away and within a half hour George was completely numb. It still hurt to walk, of course, but once his feet had frozen it wasn't so bad.

"Just gotta keep walking," George reminded himself out loud over and over again. He knew that it was only a matter of time before his feet would get so badly frozen that the frostbite would not go away and his feet would need to be chopped off. It had already happened to one soldier in the company. The very image of his friend Tony screaming as the surgeon sawed off his foot was enough to turn George's slow walk into a jog.

Allison tugged on his hand.

"Huh?" George mumbled, turning to see what she wanted. "Oh, I'm sorry," he said when he realized the problem. "Am I walking too fast?"

She nodded her head up and down.

"I'm sorry," George apologized. "I just want to get you to the aid station as fast as possible, so we can find someone to help you."

Allison's head bent down in what looked like sadness.

"What's wrong?" George asked.

She did not answer; she only looked up at him, smiled a little, and shrugged her shoulders.

"Hey," George said as he turned and began walking some more. "Would it make you feel better if I sing a song?"

Allison nodded her head up and down quickly.

"I thought so," George grinned. "It always cheers me up when we are marching from one place to another. Hmmmm, let me see." George thought for a moment then began to slowly sing: *"O, I wish I was in the land of cotton."*

Allison smiled one of the biggest smiles George had ever seen. He knew she'd like that song. "Dixie" had become the South's national anthem. It brought warm feelings of pride and sadness to every Southerner and it was also a fun song to sing. He smiled as he continued, picking up the pace as he went.

"Old times there are not forgotten Look away! Look away! Look away! Dixie Land."

As he began to sing faster the two of them began to swing their hands and walk faster to the beat of George's voice. They even skipped a little.

"O, I wish I was in Dixie! Hooray! Hooray! In Dixie Land I'll take my stand To live and die in Dixie. Away, away, away down south in Dixie! Away, away, away down south in Dixie!"

By the time they had reached the aid station, George had gone through just about every verse of "Dixie" as well as every other marching song he had ever heard. But it was all worth it. Allison had never stopped smiling, and the trip had gone by so fast that he was surprised that they had reached the aid station so soon.

"Well, here we are," he said to Allison when they were in sight of the station. It was an old church that had been left alone by both armies until the battle had forced it to become a refuge for the many families running from the destruction of Fredericksburg. But while it looked warm and cozy inside, neither Allison nor George showed any great desire to go in.

Allison looked up at him. Her eyes were sad again.

"What?" George cried in frustration. "What's wrong now?"

She just looked down.

"I got you here, didn't I?" George continued in almost a yell. "I took you where you wanted to go, didn't I? I walked miles through the snow to get you here; I gave you my new socks so you'd be warm, and now you're all sad. What is it?"

Allison looked up for a second. Her eyes were filled with tears.

"What?" George just about screamed. "What do you want? I can't help you if you don't talk?"

Allison stared down at the ground again.

"C'mon," George said in a huff. He pulled Allison by the hand and knocked on the church door.

"Yes?" the man said as he opened the door. He was dressed in a gray overcoat, and his voice was gentle and soft.

"I'm here to deliver a refugee," George said simply. He did not really look at the man as he talked. His attention was on the warm fire he could just barely see through the crack in the door.

"Hmmmm?" the man wondered, following George's eyes. "Oh, yes, of course! Come in, come in. You must be freezing."

George rushed in, dragging Allison behind. He walked straight towards the fire, slipped off his shoes, and began to rub his feet.

"Here is a little bit of food and drink," the man said after a few minutes had passed.

"Huh," George said, turning his head. He had been so intent on warming his feet that he had not noticed anyone or anything else in the room at all. "Oh, thank you," he said, reaching for the plate.

"And for you, little girl," the man continued as he handed Allison a plate as well.

"What's your name?" he said to her as she took the food and began to eat slowly.

"It's Allison," George interrupted. "She can't talk."

"Can't talk?" the man repeated.

"Or won't," George added. "I don't know. She's just all messed up. I found her yesterday in the woods and gave her some food and my socks, but she hasn't said a word to me."

"How do you know her name?" the man asked.

"We guessed it," George answered. "She can hear alright, although one of her ears has been shot off."

"My Lord," the man gasped. "What has this girl been through?"

"Beats me," George said as he took another bite of the small piece of pork left on his plate. "Like I said, she won't say a thing. I think her parents are dead and I can't figure out if she's got any friends or relatives left at all."

"Well, you've done the right thing by bringing her here," the man answered confidently. "Unfortunately, we've had lots of experience dealing with refugees and children and all kinds of problems."

George looked around the room for the first time and was surprised at how crowded it was. The church was small with only one room and half of it was taken up by the altar and the fireplace. Yet, there must have been 10 or 15 families huddled inside. There were mothers with children, some fathers, and even a few pets. Despite this chaos, it still was clear where one family ended and the next began by the way their few clothes and bags were arranged. It was as if each family had staked out their own little section of floor to serve as their new home; at least until they found a real one.

George looked at some of the other children. They expressed the same sad look in their eyes that Allison had: the look that said they felt all alone. When they walked or made gestures it was slow and awkward as if in a dream. George continued to stare. When he met the eyes of a few of the children they paid no attention to him and continued tidying up the few belongings they had left or eating some scrap of meat that they had warmed in the fire.

"Are all these people homeless?" George asked.

"Yes, I believe so," answered the man. "Most of them had their homes destroyed when the Yankees attacked the town."

"What are they doing now?" George asked softly.

"Waiting," the man replied. "Just waiting."

"For what?" George said in surprise.

"For someone to help them or to rebuild their town," answered the man. "Many people have already gone to Richmond, but these people and others like them have remained behind, either because Richmond is getting too crowded or because they just can't bear to leave the land they've called home for so long."

"How long will they wait?"

"I don't know," the man replied. "Some of them have been here for almost two months now and still we've seen no changes. Many of them have given up all hope of ever returning to a normal life."

George looked around again in silence. He couldn't believe all of the victims he'd seen hurt by the Yankees. When the call first came through the lines that soldiers were volunteering their pay to help out the refugees, George was one of the first to offer to help. It was the least he could do for the many people without homes. It was only money, he had thought when he had given up his pay. Yet, as he watched these poor refugees in silence he realized that he, his buddies, all of the soldiers, politicians, and newspaper writers could never really understand the terrible loss these people had suffered. George just couldn't imagine what it would be like to lose everything you know and love and to be left with nothing except for a small space on a cold floor in a dark church.

"Well, I suppose you should head back to your unit now," the man said suddenly, breaking George out of his thoughts. "It'll be getting dark in several hours and we wouldn't want you to get lost."

"Uh...yeah," George said slowly. He was having second thoughts about leaving Allison with these people. She would be lost among so many refugees, and no one there looked as if they had any energy to spare to help a poor, orphaned, mute girl.

"Don't worry," the man said, sensing George's reluctance. "She'll be fine with us."

George looked at Allison softly. She was still holding his hand and George realized that she had never let go, even when they were eating.

"I've got to go now, Allison," George said towards her audible ear. He placed his other hand on top of hers, so that both his hands held hers warmly. "But don't you worry. These nice people will take care of you. I promise."

George stood up to leave, but Allison had not let go.

"Please, Allison," he begged. "Don't make this any harder than it is already. You know I can't take care of you. I'm a soldier. I've got to march all over the country fighting battles and maybe even dying. That's no place for a little girl. Besides, there are rules against these things. I can't keep a girl in my tent."

Allison began to loosen her grip but did not let go.

"You'll be fine here," the man interrupted as he reached between the two and gently pulled Allison's hand away from George's. "We'll take good care of you and see that you get well fed and stay warm and maybe we can even find some shoes for you."

Allison looked down at her feet and wondered for a minute. George slipped his hand completely away. Allison reached out again but it was too late.

"Good-bye, Allison," George said softly as he kissed her on the cheek. Then, he turned away and walked out into the cold.

George walked into his tent.

"Did you do it?" Eric asked as he looked up from his bed and sat up. He had been looking over the newspaper that George had gotten the other day to try to find out anything that he could understand. Although he still couldn't read, he could look at the few pictures and make out some of the familiar words like General Lee, Yankees, and Richmond.

"Yeah," George answered in a low mumble.

"How did it go?" Eric asked, laying the paper down and stretching his arms out a little. He was pretty tired after another tedious day at guard duty. Standing around for hours seemed to make him more tired and sore than chopping wood or practicing drills.

"O.K., I guess," George continued to mumble. He sat down on the edge of his bed and began to untie his shoes. "The aid station wasn't that far away."

"Are they gonna help her?" Eric wondered.

"I guess so...maybe," George answered mysteriously.

"Maybe," Eric repeated. "What do you mean maybe?"

"I dunno," George replied, slowly pulling the shoe off his left foot. He winced as the cold air stung his skin bringing the feeling back into his toes. "They seemed to have too many other problems and people to deal with."

"What do you mean?" Eric asked as he stared down at George's feet. It was the first time he'd seen George's discolored and parched toes.

"Well, the place was filled with families who had nowhere to go," George explained, rubbing his toes to bring them back to life. "They were just living there, in the church, waiting for something to happen or for someone to come save them. But I don't think they felt anyone was ever gonna come save them. They had these long, dark faces as if they knew that there was nothing or no one that would ever help them."

Eric just stared at George, listening to every word. George continued.

"It was like I had walked into an ongoing funeral. The place was deathly quiet, and even though it was the middle of the day and the sun was shining brightly, it was dark, damp, and depressing."

"Wow," Eric whistled. "So what did you do?"

"What could I do?" George shrugged. "I had to get back to the camp and I couldn't bring Allison with me."

"Did she say anything?" Eric asked, hoping that at least this might force her to speak.

"No," George answered. "She just stared at me with those big, blue eyes of hers and held onto my hand as tight as she could. I didn't think I'd ever be able to let her go, but the pastor gently took her hand and pulled it away."

"She didn't scream or cry or nothing when you left?" Eric wondered.

"No," George said, looking down at the ground and rubbing his hands. "She groaned and grunted and as I turned I saw tears in her eyes. I needed to get out of there as fast as I could before she clung to me again."

"Must've been hard," Eric commented.

"You have no idea," George looked up at him. "Every part of me wanted to turn around, grab her, and take her away from that awful place. Twice, I almost did. I just couldn't imagine her wasting away in there, waiting for someone to come along and take care of her. If I hadn't run all the way back here I probably would have turned around."

"Gee, George," Eric began. "I'm awful sorry you had to do that."

"Yeah, me too," George answered.

The two boys sat in an awkward silence for several seconds. George continued to rub his toes, and Eric shuffled the newspaper around trying to neaten it.

"You missed the news," Eric said finally.

"What news?" George asked.

"We're moving out," Eric answered with a little bit of excitement in his voice. He never was sure how he felt at times like this. It was always nice when they were camped for awhile. You had a regular place to sleep and you usually knew what you would be doing the next day. But it also was really boring. On the other hand, when they moved out it meant that they could be marching for days or weeks at a time, never sleeping in the same place twice, and always wondering when and if a battle would suddenly begin. But at least it was more exciting.

"Where to?" George wondered.

"Don't know," Eric replied. "The captain is kinda upset cuz he doesn't wanna leave General Lee and the rest of the army, but I guess Longstreet wuz ordered to take our division off and head back towards Richmond."

"Richmond?" George cried. He couldn't contain his excitement. He hadn't been home in over a year and if they were headed in that direction maybe he might have a chance to—

The tent flap opened slowly as a small hand forced its way in. George stopped and turned his attention towards the figure entering. It was a little blond, blue-eyed girl holding a familiar armless doll.

"Allison!" George cried, standing up in surprise. "What are you doing here?"

"Huh?" Eric managed to say as he too stood up next to George.

Allison looked down at the ground and stared. George ran and hugged her.

"I never thought I'd see you again!" George said happily. He pushed Allison back a little with his hands so he could see her face. She was smiling.

"How did you get back here?" George grinned. He couldn't help it. She was so beautiful, and he had been so upset with himself after he had left her in that cold, dark church.

"Hey," George said suddenly as a wave of anger washed over him. "How did you get out of the church?"

Allison didn't say a word of course. She just continued to stare at George.

"You shouldn't have run away," George scolded. The anger, still there, was quickly draining away as he continued to look into Allison's deep-set eyes. "They're gonna worry about you."

Allison looked down a little.

"If they even notice," George went on as his anger transferred itself to the refugee center. "They were probably so busy doing nothing that they don't even know you're gone. And, of course, they won't know where to find you since I never told them my unit."

"George," Eric finally interrupted. He had been standing back a little and watching the little reunion. "What are you gonna do now?"

"Huh?" George responded.

"You know she can't stay here," Eric explained.

Allison turned towards George. Her eyes were filled with fear and worry.

"She's shivering," George noticed, ignoring Eric completely and placing Allison on his bed. "We need to warm her."

George began to rub Allison's exposed arms with his hands trying to get the blood flowing again.

"Here," he said, taking a crumbly blanket from the side. "Cover yourself with this."

"George," Eric interrupted again. "What are you gonna do?"

"Is that better?" George asked Allison in a soft voice.

"George!" Eric shouted.

George stopped what he was doing and turned towards Eric.

"What are you going to do?" Eric repeated slowly now that he finally had George's attention.

"I don't know," George answered slowly as he turned his head back and forth between Allison and Eric.

"You should take her back to the center," Eric suggested.

"No way!" George argued. "She'll rot there like the other refugees. Besides, she'll just run away again."

"Well, you can't take her with you," Eric reminded George. "We're moving out tomorrow and there's no way you can take a little girl on a hundred mile march."

"I know," George answered. He hung his head down in defeat and confusion.

"Hey wait!" he said suddenly with a gleam in his eye. "Maybe I can take her home."

"Home?" Eric repeated.

"Yeah, to Richmond," George explained as he thought out loud. "We're marching that direction any-way, right?"

"Yeah," Eric answered slowly with worry edging into his voice.

"And if I ask for a short leave I could get into the city for a few days, right?"

"Yeah."

"And if I go see my dad, I'm sure he'll help!" George's voice was almost a shout now as he began to speak faster. "He has always wanted a daughter and he's always saying he misses his nieces up North, and I know my stepmom will say O.K. She wants another daughter too and she can't say no to me after all I've done in the war."

"George," Eric tried to interrupt.

"Plus, who can turn Allison away?" he rambled.

"George."

"She's so cute and so adoring that they'll have to take her."

"George!" Eric shouted.

"What?" George shouted back.

"What about the twins and the crowds in the city and your dad's and mom's jobs?" Eric finally managed to say. "They can't afford the money or the time to take care of another child."

"Sure they can," George argued. "They have to."

Eric stared at him.

George stared back.

They both looked at Allison. She was sitting comfortably under the blankets with her big, blue eyes staring up at the two boys. She had heard everything.

"Allison," George began, turning towards her and kneeling in front of the bed. "Would you like to live with my family in Richmond?"

Allison slowly nodded her head up and down.

"Well, there you have it," George turned towards Eric and stood. "She's gonna live with my family."

"Haven't you forgotten one thing?" Eric reminded him.

"What?" George wondered.

"You still have to ask for leave," Eric said smartly. "What if they don't let you go?"

"They have to!" George shouted.

"Well, you better hurry then," Eric said. "It's almost curfew and if you don't ask today you might not get your chance before we move out."

George took a sudden, quick breath, realized Eric was right, and bolted out of the tent.

"Keep an eye on Allison!" he managed to say as he disappeared into the night.

Chapter Sixteen
Richmond, Again

Getting leave was easy. Getting home was not.

There was no railroad service between Fredericksburg and Richmond anymore, so George and Allison would have to walk. At first, the going was extremely slow, and George was afraid that they both would die of frostbite before they got halfway to Richmond. The snow was everywhere and the temperature had dropped to below zero. Fortunately, there was still enough dry wood around for George to stop and to make a fire every several miles, but that slowed them even more.

He had managed to get Allison a pair of shoes and a cover-up from donations of several soldiers in his company. They had told George that they had already given all of their pay to help the refugees, so what was a pair of shoes and a blanket by now? George had smiled and given them what remained of his stepmother's cookies and apples as a thank-you anyway. He knew how much shoes and blankets were worth.

There were refugees everywhere on the road. More than once George and Allison had to run off to the side of the road for fear of getting run over by a large family with a wagon load of supplies. They all seemed to be on their way to Richmond, and by the second day of walking, George had decided to forget his pride and began to ask the passersby whether they had any room for Allison and him on their wagon.

On the third day they found a family who had a little space for Allison. There was only room for one, however, and with Allison beginning to cough and wheeze it was obvious that she would need to ride the entire way while George walked. Allison hadn't wanted to release George's hand, but she was so weak that it was just a simple matter for George to lift her up and place her little body between a few articles of clothing in the middle of the wagon.

The cold did not ease and by the time they reached Richmond, Allison could barely stand. George also had trouble moving his legs and had to get help to lift Allison down from the wagon.

"You're sure you'll be alright?" the man asked George as he set down Allison next to him. Even though she was shaky on her feet, she still managed to grasp George's hand and stand quietly next to him.

"We'll be fine," George assured him. The familiar touch of Allison's warm hand satisfied him more than he expected, and he felt a renewal of self-confidence now that they were together again. "My house is just a short walk from here."

"Alright," the man answered. "But we'll watch you walk down the street just to be sure."

"O.K.," George agreed. "And thank-you so much for the ride. You probably saved her life."

The man looked down at Allison, who smiled softly. "Think nothing of it," he said with a wave of his hand. "We all gotta stick together till these Yankees are licked."

"Well thanks again, anyway," George said one more time as he started towards his home. "And good luck finding a place to stay."

The walk to his home was a short one; at the same time it was long enough for George to see how much

Richmond had changed. The streets were crowded with all kinds of strangers. Poor beggars, starving refugees, wounded soldiers, and the occasional policeman wandered up and down the streets. All were looking for a path through the crowds to get to wherever it was that they were going. The regular Richmond citizens stared through them or looked away completely as if they were trying to ignore how much their city had changed. The clothing everyone wore was worn and gray. The fancy gowns and sharp suits of the rich and not so rich had disappeared as all clothing had been either donated to the hospitals or to some other cause in the war against the Yankee invaders.

Auctioneers yelled over the noise, waving their red flags in the air and trying to draw the attention of the passersby to their makeshift stores set up on the side of the road. In many areas of the city, these were the only stores available. The blockade of Union ships had almost stopped all trade with the outside world. They sold anything they had managed to smuggle at unreasonably high prices. If there were no takers at the price they wanted, then they had a secret set-up man who bought the stuff for resale somewhere else in the city.

"What has happened here?" George wondered out loud. "The city used to be so beautiful and happy. Now it's like some kind of eerie ghost town filled with strange noises and strange people. It's like a nightmare."

George looked down at Allison expecting some kind of response, but she continued to blankly stare forward.

"First, they destroy your city," George said to her, "then mine."

They continued on their way down the street and into George's neighborhood, which had also changed. The laughing and playing of the children were gone now if for no other reason than there was too much traffic on the street to play. Instead, some children had set up lemonade stands to raise money for the war effort. George almost stopped and talked with one of the kids he recognized, but he realized that he needed to get Allison inside.

"It's just around the corner," he told her.

They made it through the streets relatively quickly despite the crowds. George was still wearing his uniform and he realized after a few minutes that many people would move to the side to let him pass quicker as if he were some kind of celebrity.

"Here we are," George said nervously as they stopped in front of his house. He wasn't sure what to do or say now that he was actually here. He hadn't had any time to tell anybody he was coming and he wasn't even sure if anyone would be home. His father was probably still at work. Now that his stepmother was volunteering at the hospital, she might have left the twins with someone and be out too.

George thought for a moment. *Should he knock or just go right in? It was his house after all.* He reached for the doorknob and slowly turned it.

"Hello?" George called as he poked his head into the house. "Is anyone home?"

There was no response.

"Hello-o-o," George called again. He shut the door behind him and walked into the main part of the house. Allison was still holding his hand.

"It looks like no one is home," he said to her with a shrug. "Let's get something to eat while we wait."

They walked towards the kitchen to try to find some food. George's stomach growled and his throat ached as he thought about all the wonderful food that must be waiting for him. It wasn't just that he hadn't eaten in over 8 hours. He couldn't remember the last time he had a warm meal or a good piece of meat or anything other than hardtack and coffee.

"C'mon," he urged Allison on. "I'm starving!"

They ran into the kitchen and stopped suddenly. George's stepmother was sitting at the table with her head resting on her hands, fast asleep. She stirred.

"Oh-h-h," she moaned as she lifted her head and rubbed her eyes. George stood still and waited for her eyes to focus. Her head arched when she realized someone was in the room with her. Her eyes opened wide and her jaw dropped.

"G-George?" she managed to say. "George, is that you?"

"Hi, Sallie," George said simply. A sly smile began to appear on his face. "How are you?"

"George!" she shouted as she bolted out of her chair and ran towards him. "My Lord, what are you doing here? We had no idea you were coming home. Is everything O.K.? Are you injured?"

"I'm fine, I'm fine," George laughed. "I was granted leave last week so I could bring Allison here."

"Allison?" Sallie repeated, looking down for the first time at the little girl holding George's hand. "I don't understand."

"Allison," George began formally, "meet my step-mother, Sallie. Sallie, this is Allison. She is an orphan I found wandering in the woods outside of Fredericksburg."

"Oh my," Sallie gasped with both hands covering her mouth. She bent down to look Allison in the eyes. "Hello, Allison," she said, taking Allison's hand and shaking it gently. "It's nice to meet you."

"She can't talk, Sallie," George explained when Allison gave no response. "She also can only hear on her left side. Her right ear has been shot off."

"Oh, you poor dear," Sallie cried as she pulled Allison towards her and gave her a hug. The girl did not resist but she did not return the hug either. She just kind of stood there, waiting for Sallie to finish.

"She's warm, George," Sallie said suddenly in a worried and concerned voice. She pushed Allison back a little and placed her hand on the girl's forehead. "Is she sick?"

"I'm not sure," George answered honestly. "She has been weak and pale ever since we left camp for Richmond. I figured it was just the cold."

"It could be," Sallie replied as she thought out loud, "but it could also be worse. I've seen lots of cases of smallpox at the hospital lately, especially in the Fredericksburg refugees."

"Smallpox?" George repeated loudly.

"Don't worry yet, George," Sallie said, trying to calm him down. "It could just be the cold like you said. But we better get her warmed up, fed, and in bed just in case. Why don't you go to your room and get your bed together. It's still exactly the way you left it."

George smiled a little. He was glad to hear that Sallie had not taken advantage of his room and had given it to some refugee or had donated the sheets to the hospital. He had been afraid that as soon as he left for the war that she would erase all evidence of him living there like the wicked stepmother in that fairy tale he read in school once.

"O.K.," George agreed. He turned towards his room and left the kitchen. Allison broke free of Sallie and raced after him. George picked her up and held her.

"Wanna see my room?" he asked her with a smile.

She grinned and nodded her head up and down. George laughed a little and continued on to his room.

"George!" Sallie called before he had completely left her sight. "Welcome home!"

CHAPTER SEVENTEEN
THE FEVER

George knelt next to the bed and placed another cloth on Allison's forehead. The fever had definitely gotten worse in the few hours since he had arrived. Allison was already moaning and whining in bed; she hadn't even eaten the food that Sallie had prepared to celebrate George's return.

"I'm really worried about her, Sallie," George said, turning towards his stepmother who was standing over the bed.

"Me too, George," she said softly. "I've seen too many people die in the past year. Every time it happens I feel like a little part of me has died too."

George didn't say a word. He just frowned.

"But don't worry yet," Sallie suddenly reassured him. "Richmond has the finest doctors in the country. Even though I've seen my share of death, most of the patients that get treated in time survive and are released."

George grunted but still did not say anything. He turned back towards Allison and stroked her hair.

"Such fine, beautiful hair," Sallie commented.

"Mmmm," George agreed.

"Sallie?" a voice called from the other room.

"In here, dear," Sallie called to George's father. She turned towards George with a smile and held her finger to her lips. "Shhhh," she whispered.

George smiled and stood up behind Sallie.

"What are you doing in here?" George's father asked as he walked into the room.

"Hi, Dad," George said with a casual wave of his hand as he stood out from behind Sallie.

"George?" he said softly. "George!" he shouted and ran towards his son, grabbing him with both arms and squeezing so tight that George gasped for air. "George!" he shouted again in complete joy.

"D-dad, dad," George groaned. "I can't breathe."

"Hah...sorry, son," his father chuckled as he loosened his grip and stood back a little to look at his son. He gave him another hug, this time much gentler. George hugged him back.

"It's good to see you, Dad," George said.

"My Lord, it's good to see you too, son," his father answered.

"Hey, George," a voice called from behind his father. George looked in the direction of the sound.

"John?" George said. Even though John was a friend of the family, George was surprised to see a black boy standing in his house this late at night.

"John has been coming here on a regular basis ever since the war began," George's father explained when he saw the look of confusion on George's face. "With you gone and Sallie volunteering in the hospital, we've had no time to get any chores done around the house. If John hadn't offered to help out, I don't know what we would have done."

"Oh," George said simply. He felt a mixture of gratitude that John would be so willing to help his family and jealousy as if John was somehow taking George's place.

"Who's the girl?" John asked, trying to change the direction of the conversation.

"She's an orphan from Fredericksburg," George answered as he turned his attention back towards Allison and began stroking her hair again. "I brought her here because I didn't know what else to do with her, but I think the trip may have been too much."

"I think she may have smallpox, Sean," Sallie whispered to her husband.

Sean nodded slowly and placed his hand on his chin to think. "Well, it seems we have a lot to talk about, son," he said after a few seconds. "John, would you keep an eye on the girl while we go in the other room and get caught up?"

"Certainly, sir," John answered.

George stroked Allison's hair one last time and then got up slowly. He handed John the damp cloth. "She likes it when you stroke her hair," George reminded him. "And she can only hear on her left side."

"O.K.," John replied as he took the cloth and kneeled next to Allison.

"C'mon, son," George's father said as he put his arm around his son's shoulder. "Let's get reacquainted."

They talked for hours. George discussed life in the army, the battles he had seen, the friends he had made, and the destruction of Fredericksburg. He made sure to thank Sallie over and over again for the care package that she had sent several months ago. He told her about every soldier who ate one of her cookies and what they said. Sallie laughed and promised to make more.

George's father explained the work he had been doing in the iron factory and of all the weapons they had tried to make for the army. George tried to pay attention when he started talking about all the politics that were going on in the factory and in the city, but it was getting late and the trip and the excitement of coming home were finally catching up with him.

"You're drifting off, son," his father finally said. "Why don't you go to bed?"

"I bet it will feel nice to be in your own room again," Sallie said with a smile.

"Do we have any extra blankets or pillows?" Sean asked Sallie.

"Oh no," Sallie said with a look of concern. "I gave them all to the hospital."

"Don't worry," George reassured her. "I'm a soldier now. I'll sleep on the floor next to Allison."

"You sure?" Sean asked his son.

"Don't worry, Dad," George repeated. "After all I've been through I could sleep on a bed of rocks."

Chapter Eighteen
Spies

"Have you found out anything?" the well-dressed black boy said to John from the darkness of the shadows.

"Not yet," John answered. He looked up and down the street and then ducked into the alley. Even though it was not yet curfew, he knew that two black boys talking in this part of town would arouse suspicion.

"But it has been over a week," the other boy said. "Hasn't he said anything at all about his unit."

"It has been hard to get him to talk," John answered. "He's so worried about the girl that he doesn't talk much and when he does, it's about her."

"Well, you better find out something soon," the other boy warned. "We've gotta leave in a couple of days, and Mary wants to pass on some more information to the Yankee man before we go."

"Leave?" John repeated.

"Yeah, dummy," the boy answered quickly. He looked nervously to his left and right again as if he was about to say something he was afraid others would hear. "We're escaping up North, remember?"

"Yeah," John said with a smile. His mind flashed back to several months ago when the word first became known about the Emancipation Proclamation. President Lincoln finally had decided to free what slaves he could. More importantly for John, Lincoln also had decided to let blacks fight in the Union army. John had become tired of spying on George's family. He felt somewhat ashamed even though he knew he was doing it for a good cause. George and Sean had always treated him fairly, better than most other whites, and even though the information he gathered at the weapons factory was important, he really never felt comfortable being a spy. So when he heard that his friends were planning an escape up North to join the black regiments that were forming, he was one of the first to sign up.

"So you gotta find out something from this George guy tonight," John's friend reminded him. "The rest of us are leaving and we want you with us. Understand?"

"Yeah," John answered, nodding his head. "Don't worry. I'll be there."

John turned, looked to his left and right, and then slipped into the street. He pulled the loaf of bread out of his shirt that George had sent him to find, then headed back towards George's house. As long as he walked straight ahead and made it clear that he had somewhere to go, he would be left alone. The whites only bothered the blacks when they were hanging around or walking the streets aimlessly.

"Here you go," John said with a smile as he handed George the loaf of bread through the open door.

"Come in, come in," George urged him rudely as he pulled John into the house and shut the door. "We've got a problem."

"A problem?" John repeated.

"Yeah," George answered. He led John into the room where Allison was still resting and knelt beside her again. Her face was as white as the snow that still fell around the city, and her body had lost most of its weight from lack of food. Once in awhile she opened her eyes to seemingly recognize George; however, she would just moan and quickly fall asleep again. She had been like that for over a week now. A doctor had come finally to see her after Sallie begged a friend at work. Unfortunately, he had not been able to do anything for Allison. After looking carefully at her—checking her temperature and examining her sores—he could only tell them that they would have to wait and see whether she lived or died. George had refused to accept that and so he had stayed by her side practically every minute of the day. He brushed her hair, gave her water, and even sang to her. His only relief was when John showed up to help out.

"I've been called back to my regiment," George said to John as he continued brushing Allison's hair and staring at her face.

"Your regiment?" John repeated. He felt a mixture of worry and excitement. Maybe he finally would learn something worth passing on. "Where is it?"

"They're outside the city," George answered. "And I've got to get back."

"But what about Allison?" John wondered.

"You're gonna have to watch over her," George answered. His back faced John as he continued to stare at Allison's face. John could not see the tears that began to form around George's eyes.

"Me?" John almost shouted. "Why me?"

"Cuz you're the only one who has been around her this past week," George explained. "My dad and stepmom have been too busy working to be home much, and Allison needs someone who she knows to keep her comfortable."

"But what about my job at the iron works?" John protested. He was beginning to panic. If George made him stay, he would miss the meeting, his friends would run up North to fight without him, and he would be stuck in Richmond all by himself.

"My dad can cover for you," George answered simply. "He's your boss, remember?"

"But George," John whined softly. He struggled to come up with an excuse.

"Listen, John," George said angrily. He finally had turned and stood to face John. Tears were streaming down his face. "Sometimes you gotta do things you don't wanna do. You think I want to leave Allison? You think I want to run off into the cold, fight in battles, and maybe die while she sits here and withers away into nothing? Look at her!" he shouted.

"Look at her!" he shouted again and pointed. "She's just a little girl. A little girl! Her mommy and daddy are dead. Her house and city have been destroyed. Her ear has been shot off and she's so confused and upset that she can't even talk."

John stared down at Allison as he listened to George. He couldn't help but feel sorry for her. She obviously was a white girl and he was a slave but John didn't see that now. She was just a little girl, struggling to survive in this terrible world, and he was the only one who could help her.

"I don't want to leave her," George continued. "Lord, every part of my body is screaming to forget the war, forget my duties, and stay here to take care of her. But I can't. I have to go. I have to fight, kill, march, and run. I can't just stay here because it's what I want to do."

Allison moaned. George spun around and knelt next to her. She moaned again and opened her eyes.

"Allison?" George said softly and quickly as he stroked her hair. "Allison?"

She smiled at him.

"How do you feel?" George asked.

She frowned. Her eyes closed for a second.

"Want some water?" George asked eagerly.

She nodded. George gently lifted the glass up to her lips.

"I've got to go, Allison," he said suddenly. His stomach began to tighten and his throat became dry.

Allison's eyes opened wide and she began to shake her head back and forth, faster and faster.

"The regiment has called me b-b-back," George continued. He struggled to hold in the tears and to remain calm. If he was going to say good-bye he had to make it quick. "John will take care of you. He's real nice and I'm sure you'll like him."

She continued to shake her head back and forth. She knocked the glass of water away from George's hand and it crashed to the floor.

"Please don't be angry," George begged. "I have to go. If I don't, the Yankees will win the war and ruin everything."

Allison continued to protest. George kissed her on the forehead and stood up.

"Take good care of her, John," he said.

George looked back at Allison, who was still shaking her head, as he walked towards the door.

"George!" a shrill, dry voice suddenly screamed. George turned back towards the bed. It was Allison! She talked!

"George!" she screamed again. "Don't go!"

George turned and ran back to Allison's side.

"Allison!" he cried. "You can talk, you can talk!" George felt like celebrating. His heart was suddenly light again, and the smile on his face was so large it hurt.

"George, don't go," Allison said again.

George was still smiling, forgetting for the moment that he had to go and thinking only of Allison's talking.

"She can talk!" George said turning to John. "She can talk."

John smiled. It really was an amazing thing.

"George, don't go," Allison said again.

"I have to," George answered slowly. All the joy left him again as his heart came crashing down. Even this wonderful event could not stop the war. Nothing could stop the war. He had to go.

"Please understand," George begged, "I don't want to go. I want to stay with you and take care of you, but I have to do my duty. I'm a soldier now."

"George, don't go," Allison repeated.

"John will take care of you," George said. He kissed Allison on the forehead one last time.

"Good-bye, Allison," George said softly. No tears came this time. George felt weak and drained and cold.

"Take care of her, John," he mumbled.

"I will, George," John promised. He no longer worried about the meeting. He no longer worried about the war. It could wait. He had something more important to do now, something that had nothing to do with slavery or secession or war. He had to take care of a little girl.

CHAPTER NINETEEN
FATHER AND SON

George ran out of the room. Allison's words were ringing in his ears. *Stop it, stop it, stop it,* he told himself. *Stop thinking about her. It's time to be a soldier now. You never cried when your friends got shot. You never cried when you saw them being blown apart by a cannon.*

George began to feel angry. *Why did the Yankees have to go and start this whole thing in the first place?* he thought bitterly. *And why did he have to go off to fight and leave his family. He didn't own slaves. He didn't even like slavery. But the whole thing blew up in his face anyway and now he was stuck in the middle.*

"Look out, son," Sean warned as George almost ran into him. His father grabbed him by both arms and looked him in the face. "Where are you off to in such a hurry?"

"Dad!" George cried. "I was afraid I wouldn't get a chance to see you."

"No chance of that, son," his father replied. "I heard through the grapevine at work that your regiment was on the move and I came over immediately."

"Dad, Allison can talk!" George cried suddenly changing the topic.

"What?" his father said, looking past George and towards the room she was in.

"She can talk!" George repeated. "I was saying good-bye to her and she yelled: 'George, don't go; George, don't go!'"

"Well, I'll be d——d," his father swore.

"But I couldn't stay, Dad," George continued. "I had to leave her there crying out my name for the first time, and go off to rejoin the regiment."

"I'm sorry, son," his father said softly.

"It's just not fair," George yelled. "I took such good care of her. I gave her my new socks; I gave her my food; I took her where she needed to go; I stayed by her side all this time; and now when she finally says my name I have to go."

"I know, son," his father said, "and I'm sorry."

"It's just so stupid," George went on. "Why did they have to pick on a little girl? Why did they have to go and destroy so much. I thought this war was just going to be a fight between soldiers, not kids and little girls."

"So did I," his father answered. "So did everyone. But look at you, son. You're no old man yourself."

George looked at his father in confusion.

"You're still my son," he explained, "still only 14 years old. Still just a boy."

George started to protest, but his father held up his hand.

"No, no," he argued. "I know you're not a boy anymore. You left here as a boy, still wondering about how you were going to make friends and when your next fight would be. It was all just a big adventure to you."

George smiled a little, remembering how excited he was when he first went off to fight.

"But look at you now," his father continued. "You're not a boy anymore. You don't have that smile, that innocent look. Your eyes are dark and your thoughts are angry."

"I didn't mean to change," George said simply.

"I know," his father reassured him. "You just wanted to do what you thought was right and have some fun while you were at it."

George smiled again as he thought of how he had been.

"But I'm proud of you, son," his father continued. "You stuck through all this, helped out your friends, and became a good soldier."

George looked at his dad and realized for the first time that he no longer was staring up at his face. Their eyes were level.

"But you also became a good man," he said. "You took care of this little girl, nursed her back to health, and sacrificed your time and your personal clothing to take care of her." He paused while he looked at his son. "I love you, son," he said as he grabbed George and gave him a big hug. George hugged him back. It was a tight, warm hug. The kind of hug his dad used to give him when he woke up in the morning. It made him feel welcome and loved and protected. He didn't want to let go. They hugged in silence for several minutes.

"I have to go, Dad," George said finally.

"I know," his father answered as he let go.

"Take care of the family and Allison," George said.

"Don't worry," his father answered. "I will. You just take care of yourself and keep your head down. O.K.?"

"O.K.," George smiled. He turned and walked towards the door.

"George," his father called one last time.

George stopped and turned around.

"I'm proud of you, son," his father said warmly.

George smiled and walked out the door.

George went off to fight again; however, this time it was very different. This time, there was no joy in his heart. There was no smile on his face and no eagerness in his stride. This time, there was only anger. He was angry at the Union soldiers who had destroyed the land. He was angry at the Union government for starting the war, and he was angry at the whole world for ruining his life.

He wasn't a boy anymore. He wasn't really a man either. He was a soldier now. He would fight and march and eat hardtack and coffee. He would die for his friends and his state, but he would never laugh at silly jokes or play in the yard or do all the other fun things he had done before this all began. His childhood was dead.

He would get back at them. He would get back at them all. If it took all of his strength and all of his determination, he would find a way to retaliate. The regiment would welcome him back with open arms and he would be the perfect soldier. He would fight until he could fight no more and he would win.

"To hell with them Yankees," George said as he closed the door of his father's house and headed back to his friends. "This war ain't even begun."

148

"This war is a joke," Joey said angrily. He had lived in the North all his life and still he couldn't understand why so many of his friends had gone to fight for Lincoln. "It all started because Lincoln wouldn't let the Southerners do what they wanted, and then you idiots run off and join up just 'cause he asks us to."

"We joined to defend our country!" Thomas yelled back. He was beginning to get angry. It was one thing to criticize the way the war was fought, but it was a completely different story to make fun of him and his family and friends who had risked their lives to join up.

"What country?" Joey replied. "The United States of America? We ain't United any more. We are the conquering states of America. We march down South and tell them people that they have to be part of our country when they don't want to."

"They can't just leave," Thomas argued.

"Why not?" Joey retorted. "They joined on their own. Why can't they leave on their own?"

"Because they can't," Thomas answered quickly. He could think of nothing else to say. It had always seemed so obvious to him. It was in the Constitution. It was the law of the land. *How could a state just quit*

the United States of America once it had joined? It
couldn't. The country would just fall apart.

"Oh good answer," Peter interrupted. "You learn
that one in that school you went to?"

"Shut up, Peter," Thomas said boldly. His face had
turned beet red and his arms had begun to shake. He
had had enough of this argument and these boys. For
years now they had been making fun of him and teas-
ing him and picking on him. He had never been able to
fight back because there was always more of them and
they were all bigger. But now, things had changed.
Thomas was not only almost as tall as them, but he
also had experienced war. He had felt what it was like
to have people trying to kill him. Compared to that,
Bobby, Peter, and Joey didn't look so threatening anymore. They just made him angry.

"Make me," Peter challenged.

Thomas swung his fist as hard and as fast as he
could. The sudden move caught Peter off guard allow-
ing Thomas to hit him squarely in the nose. Blood
started to pour down Peter's cheeks.

"You little...," Peter cussed as he lunged at Thomas.

"Get him, Pete!" Joey and Bobby yelled.

Thomas dodged out of the way and Peter went
stumbling into the dirt.

"I learned a few things in the army," Thomas
grinned. Peter got up and rushed again.

"Raarrr!" Peter cried.

Thomas dodged again, but this time Peter was able
to catch his foot and to knock Thomas off balance.
Then he jumped on top of Thomas and began punch-
ing him in the stomach. Each blow knocked the breath
out of Thomas just like when he had almost drowned.

The two boys continued to roll on the dirt together,
trading blows and yelling at each other. Joey and Bobby
stood by and watched.

"Get him, Peter, get him!" they chanted.

Thomas managed to wriggle free and stood up panting.

"Had enough?" he challenged Peter. *It really felt good to finally be able to hold his own against these guys. At least the army had been good for something,* Thomas thought.

"No way," Peter answered. He held his fists in front of his face, but his legs were shaky and he stumbled a bit.

Thomas swung hard: a left and a right and another left. Peter's head fell back with each blow to the face and then he fell to the ground, bruised and bleeding. Thomas stood over him smiling. His arms were at his side and he felt great.

"Hey," Joey said suddenly, pointing to the arm brace, now torn, that Thomas had been wearing. "Your arm is fine!"

"He ain't wounded!" Bobby shouted.

Thomas looked at his arm. It was perfectly healthy. The only thing left of his brace was a few rags hanging from his elbow. His stomach sank as he realized his secret came out.

"You lied!" Peter said, wiping the blood off his face and starting to sit up. "You ain't never been wounded."

Thomas started to back up, shaking his head back and forth, unable to say a word.

"You liar!" Bobby yelled.

"Liar!" Peter and Joey joined in.

Thomas turned and ran. Everybody would know the secret and nothing would ever be the same again.

BIBLIOGRAPHY

Beale, Jane Howison. *The Journal of Jane Howison Beale.* Fredericksburg: Historic Fredericksburg Foundation, 1995.

Bell, Michael Everette, Ph.D. *Richmond's History.* Http:// www.saturn.vcu.edu/~mebell/richmond/index.html; August 28, 1999.

Bowen, John. *Civil War Days.* London: Chartwell Books, 1987.

Boyer, Paul S., and others. *The Enduring Vision: A History of the American People.* Lexington, Mass.: D. C. Heath, 1990.

Catton, Bruce. *Hayfoot, Strawfoot: The Civil War Soldier American Heritage.* New York: American Heritage, April 1957.

Channing, Steven A. *Confederate Ordeal: The Civil War Series.* Alexandria, Va.: Time Life Books, 1984.

Dabney, Virginius. *Richmond, The Story of a City.* Charlottesville: University of Virginia Press, 1990.

Editors of Time Life Books. *Voices of the Civil War: Fredericksburg.* Alexandria, Va.: Time Life Books, 1984.

Fredericksburg Order of Battle, Army of Northern Virgina. Http://www.civilwarhome.com/anvfredericksburg.htm; September 13, 1999.

Furgurson, Ernest B. *Ashes of Glory: Richmond at War.* New York: Vintage Books, 1996.

Good, Jim. A Telephone Conversation Between the Historian at the National Park Service and Author regarding the Battle of Fredericksburg. 1999.

Goolrick, John T. *Historic Fredericksburg.* Richmond: Whittet & Shepperson, 1922.

Goolrick, William K. *Rebels Resurgent: The Civil War Series.* Alexandria, Va.: Time Life Books, 1984.

Gordon, Lesley J. *General George E. Pickett in Life and Legend.* Chapel Hill: University of North Carolina Press, 1998.

Handout on Mary Bowser. Richmond: Black History and Cultural Center of Virginia, 1999.

Hart, Albert Bushnell. *American History Told by Contemporaries, Volume IV.* New York: The Macmillan Company, 1964.

Horrocks, Thomas. "The Know Nothings." In *American History.* Vol. 1, art. 25. Guilford, Conn.: The Dushkin Publishing Group Inc., 1987.

Light, Rebecca Campbell. *War at Our Doors: The Civil War Diaries of the Bernard Sisters of Virginia.* Fredericksburg: The American History Company, 1998.

Longstreet Chronicles, The. Http://www.chickasaw.com/~rainbow/m_sdoc31.htm; December 6, 1999.

Longstreet, Lieutenant General James. *Battle of Fredericksburg, Virginia. Report of Lieut. Gen. James Longstreet, C.S.A.* Http://www.civilwarhome.com/longfredericksburg.htm; September 13, 1999.

Marye's Heights. Http://www.civilwar.org/maryes.htm; The Civil War Trust, 1999.

Massey, Mary Elizabeth. *Refugee Life in the Confederacy.* Baton Rouge: Louisiana State University Press, 1964.

McCutcheon, Marc. *Everyday Life in the 1800s.* Cincinnati: Writer's Digest Books, 1993.

McPherson, James M. *Battle Cry of Freedom.* New York: Oxford University Press, 1988.

Murphy, Jim. *The Boys' War.* New York: Clarion Books, 1990.

O'Shea, Richard, and David Greenspan. *American Heritage: Battle Maps of the Civil War.* New York: Smithmark, 1992.

Putnam, Sallie B. *Richmond During the War: Four Years of Personal Observation.* New York: G. W. Carleton & Co., 1883.

Robertson, James I. *Tenting Tonight: The Civil War Series.* Alexandria, Va.: Time Life Books, 1984.

Stevens, Joseph E. *1863: The Rebirth of a Nation.* New York: Bantam Books, 1999.

Wallace, Charles M. *Boy Gangs of Old Richmond in the Dear Old Days.* Publisher unknown. Supplied to author by the Valentine Museum, Richmond, Va., 1938.

Wallace, Lee A. *A Guide to Virginia Military Organizations, 1861–1865.* Lynchburg, Va.: H. E. Howard, 1986.